ACTIVE SPIRITUALITY

A

NON-DEVOTIONAL

GUIDE

ACTIVE SPIRITUALITY

A
NON-DEVOTIONAL
GUIDE

Charles R. Swindoll

WORD PUBLISHING
Dallas•London•Vancouver•Melbourne

ACTIVE SPIRITUALITY: A NON-DEVOTIONAL GUIDE

Portions of this book were previously published in the two volume work
entitled LIVING BEYOND THE DAILY GRIND: REFLECTIONS OF THE SONGS
AND SAYINGS OF SCRIPTURE (Books I and II). Copyright © 1988 by
Charles R. Swindoll.

Unless otherwise indicated, Scripture quotations used in this book are
from the New American Standard Bible, © 1960, 1962, 1963, 1968, 1971,
1972, 1973, 1975, 1977 by The Lockman Foundation. Used by permission.

Other Scripture quotations are from the following sources: The King
James Version of the Bible (KJV). The New Testament in Modern English
(PHILLIPS) by J. B. Phillips, published by The Macmillan Company, ©
1965 Zondervan Publishing House. *The Living Bible* (TLB), copyright 1971
by Tyndale House Publishers, Wheaton, IL. Used by permission. The
Good News Bible, Today's English Version (TEV)—Old Testament: Copy-
right © American Bible Society 1966, 1971, 1976. The Modern Language
Bible (MLB), The Berkeley Version in Modern English. Copyright © 1945,
1959, 1969 by Zondervan Publishing House. Used by permission. The
Holy Bible, New International Version (NIV). Copyright © 1973, 1978,
1984 International Bible Society. Used by permission of Zondervan Bible
Publishers.

Library of Congress Cataloging-in-Publication Data:

Swindoll, Charles R.
    Active spirituality.
    1. Bible O.T. Proverbs—Meditations. 2.   Christian   life—Biblical
teaching. I. Title
ISBN   0-8499-1169-9

4 5 6 7 8 9 0 1   BVG   9 8 7 6 5 4 3 2 1

Printed in the United States of America

∾

It is with deep feelings of gratitude
that I dedicate this volume to the men
who served on the faculty at Dallas Theological
Seminary during my years of training from 1959 to 1963.

Their competent scholarship, insightful instruction,
unfailing dedication to Christ as Lord, and relentless
commitment to the Scriptures as the inerrant
Word of God have marked me for life.

∾

Contents

Introduction   *xiii*
1   *Divine Perspective*   1
2   *Obedience*   9
3   *Depth*   17
4   *Serenity*   23
5   *A Sensitive Heart*   33
6   *Biblical Literacy*   43
7   *Friendly Counsel*   53
8   *A Controlled Tongue*   61
9   *Contentment*   71
10 *Resisting Temptation*   79
11 *Diligence*   87
12 *Submission to Sovereignty*   95
13 *Industriousness*   103
14 *Balance*   111
15 *Acceptance*   117
16 *Forgiveness*   125
17 *Affirmation*   133
18 *Tolerance*   141
19 *Taking Responsibility*   149
20 *Financial Accountability*   157
21 *Pleasing God*   169
22 *Gaining Wisdom*   176
    Conclusion   185
    Notes   191

Introduction

❀ SPIRITUALITY IS A hot topic today. Polls indicate a new interest in just about anything that promises instant spiritual transformation. Surprised? We shouldn't be. Secularism has left us morally and spiritually bankrupt. In such a failed culture, is it any wonder that there is a groundswell of interest in things spiritual? People everywhere are asking questions about God, meaning and purpose.

New beliefs and new ideas about spirituality abound. In early 1994, the *New York Times* religious bestseller list included no less than eight separate books on the subject of angels! Unfortunately, most of this material is written by people who have very little knowledge of what the Bible teaches on these subjects.

Christians, too, like no time in recent history, are being drawn to spirituality. They are trading in their old-fashioned activism of the '70s and '80s for a new-fashioned emphasis on the spiritual life. While I will be the first to applaud any "quiet revolution" that leads people back to an increase in their prayer and devotional lives, there is the ever-present danger that such a movement will lead to spiritual isolationism. Retreating from cultural and spiritual warfare makes sense only if we do so with a goal of regrouping for a counter-attack.

To those running from the trenches to the safety of a spiritual cloister, the title of this book, *Active Spirituality*, would seem like an oxymoron—something self-contradictory. But I assure you, it is not. Grounding our spiritual feet in the reality of this world is precisely what the gospel is all about.

For many years, I have taught that the Christian life is characterized by both a *vertical* perspective and horizontal *active* one. We must know both *who* we are in Christ and *how* to relate to our fellow human beings.

As always, Scripture provides us with wise sayings to help us maintain this vital balance. David's brilliant son, Solomon, the man of wisdom, left in his legacy one axiom after another which, when applied, gives us the wisdom we need to practice active spirituality. These sayings are known as proverbs.

Interestingly, the original term proverbs is a Latin derivative, meaning "to represent something." It conveys the thought of similarity: *pro*, meaning "for" or "in the place of" and *verba* meaning "words." A proverb, therefore, is a statement in the place of many words . . . a crisp saying, briefly stated, given to regulate our lives. The Book of Proverbs is a rich treasure house of short sentences drawn from long experiences.

When they are woven into the fabric of our call to active spirituality, it is remarkable how much oil they add to our gears. In fact, I am convinced it is vital that we spend time pondering and applying these wise works and timeless principles.

To help make them stick, try not to digest too great a meal in one sitting. These proverbs are like rich food, to be eaten slowly. Too much, too fast would be counterproductive. That is why I have limited our study to only twenty-two of the sayings—but sayings selected with great care. Taken as a whole, they provide a comprehensive picture of what the active spiritual life should look like. Coupled with the *Spirituality In Action* section provided for each chapter, this volume becomes very practical indeed.

Before getting under way, I must pause and express my gratitude to Byron Williamson, Kip Jordon and Joey Paul of Word Publishing. These men provided me with the inspiration and guidance to revise and update material found in my earlier two-volume work *Living Beyond the Daily Grind*. The book you hold in your hand is the result of that effort. They are my friends whose sincere affirmation fueled my fire. Along with them I thank Beverly Phillips (my editor on the original version) and Vic Strite (my editor on this new edition). And then I also want to mention Helen Peters, my diligent and committed secretary, who though now retired, has worked alongside me with each of my books.

And now . . . let's press on. My desire is that you will gain a realistic picture of the spiritual life at work, and that you will begin to apply that knowledge to your life in practical ways. Let's get started. We have an exciting journey ahead. My great hope is that this "Non-Devotional Guide" will become the catalyst you need to activate true spirituality.

1

Divine Perspective

The proverbs of Solomon the son of David,
  king of Israel:
To know wisdom and instruction,
To discern the sayings of understanding,
To receive instruction in wise behavior,
Righteousness, justice and equity;
To give prudence to the naïve,
To the youth knowledge and discretion,
A wise man will hear and increase in learning,
And a man of understanding will acquire
  wise counsel,
To understand a proverb and a figure,
The words of the wise and their riddles.
The fear of the Lord is the beginning
  of knowledge;
Fools despise wisdom and instruction.
Hear, my son, your father's instruction,
And do not forsake your mother's teaching;
Indeed, they are a graceful wreath to
  your head,
And ornaments about your neck. (1:1–9)

✿ EVERY WAKING moment of our lives we operate from one of two viewpoints: human or divine. I sometimes refer to these as horizontal perspective and vertical perspective. The more popular of the two is human; the more fruitful of the two is divine. We much prefer to think, maintain our attitudes, and conduct our lives independently. Human opinions influence us more than God's commands and principles. Horizontal solutions seem to give us greater security and pleasure, unfortunately, than vertical ones. For example, when under the gun of some deadline, we much prefer a tangible way out than God's telling us to trust Him to see us through. Rather than waiting on our Lord to solve our dilemma in His own time, we would normally choose the option of stepping in and manipulating a fast, painless escape. But by doing so, the divine process is reversed.

Active spirituality begins with God. It is grounded in divine perspective. Before we can put feet to our faith we must first see things as God sees them. That is how we begin to know God's will for our lives. The Book of Proverbs describes this spiritual condition as "to know wisdom" (1:2).

This "knowledge" is not passive. It is "working knowledge," knowledge with feet, grounded in reality, yet quick to do, to run the race, to be visible.

Because Proverbs is full of this kind of divine wisdom, yet packed with practical counsel, we will discover what active spirituality really looks like. We will discover what the characteristics are of a person whose life is balanced by the horizontal and the vertical perspectives (even though the human viewpoint comes so naturally). The good news is this: The more we pore over the sayings in Scripture, the more clearly that person comes into view. But before I say more about that, let's get a good grasp on the Book of Proverbs as a whole.

Without a doubt, Solomon's sayings offer the most practical, down-to-earth instruction in all the Bible. The entire book of thirty-one chapters is filled with capsules of truth . . . short, pithy maxims that help us face and, in fact, apply God's wisdom in real-life situations. These sayings convey specific truth in such a pointed, easily understood manner; we have little difficulty grasping the message.

The most commonly employed style of expression in Proverbs is the "couplet" . . . two ideas placed next to each other. Take Proverbs 13:10 for example:

Through presumption comes nothing but strife,
But with those who receive counsel is wisdom.

Interestingly, in Proverbs there are three main categories of couplets: contrastive, completive, and comparative.

In the contrastive couplet, the key term is usually *but*. One statement is set in contrast to the other statement, and *but* links the statements together; however, it separates the two ideas.

A wise son accepts his father's discipline,
But a scoffer does not listen to rebuke. (13:1)

Poverty and shame will come to him who
    neglects discipline,
But he who regards reproof will be honored. (13:18)

He who spares his rod hates his son,
But he who loves him disciplines him
    diligently. (13:24)

In the completive couplets, the second statement completes the first. In these couplets, the key connecting links are usually *and* or *so*.

The heart knows its own bitterness,
And a stranger does not share its joy. (14:10)

Even in laughter the heart may be in pain,
And the end of joy may be grief. (14:13)

Commit your works to the Lord,
And your plans will be established. (16:3)

In the comparative couplets, the one statement serves as a comparison of the other. In such cases, the keys to look for are *"better . . . than"* and *"as . . . so"* or *"like . . . so."*

> Better is a little with the fear of the Lord,
> Than great treasure and turmoil with it. (15:16)

> It is better to live in a corner of the roof
> Than in a house shared with a contentious
>   woman. (25:24)

Very picturesque. Often the comparative sayings are the most graphic.

While we are getting better acquainted with the ancient sayings, I should mention that this is also a book full of various kinds of people. Years ago I did an in-depth analysis of Proverbs and was surprised to discover that the book includes over 180 types of people. No wonder it is so helpful when it comes to giving wise counsel for putting our spiritual lives into action.

The major question is this: Why has God preserved these sayings down through the centuries? If we go back to the opening words of the book, we'll find the answer to that question. You might want to glance back over Proverbs 1:1–9.

As I read those words, I find five reasons God gave us this book of wisdom:

1   *To give reverence and obedience to the heart.* "The proverbs of Solomon the son of David, king of Israel:

To know wisdom and instruction" (1:1–2).

These sayings bring God into proper focus. They help us look at life from God's point of view. They assist us in knowing how to "read" God's reproofs. The Proverbs will help make our hearts obedient.

2   *To provide discernment to the eye.* "To discern the sayings of understanding" (1:2).

Discern is a crucial term. It means (in the original Hebrew verb) "to separate, to make distinct." The whole idea of giving insight is in Solomon's mind. Proverbs provides us with the ability to distinguish truth from error.

3   *To develop alertness in the walk.* "To receive instruction in wise behavior, / Righteousness, justice and equity" (1:3).

The original term translated *receive* carries with it the thought of mobility . . . taking something along with you, carrying something. In this case, what the student of God's sayings carries with him (or her) is "instruction in wise behavior." We glean from the proverbs an alertness in our daily walk. The sayings assist us when we are on the move. They help us "keep on truckin'!"

4   *To establish discretion and purpose in life.* "To give prudence to the naïve, / To the youth knowledge and discretion" (1:4).

Isn't it interesting that the dual objects of verse 4 are the naïve and the young? Those who are wide open to everything, who have little knowledge of danger—those who are gullible. Solomon assures us that these sayings will add substance and purpose to our lives.

For all those who wander aimlessly, lacking purpose and embracing merely a human viewpoint of existence, there is hope!

5 *To cultivate keenness of mind.* "To understand a proverb and a figure, / The words of the wise and their riddles" (1:6).

Finally, these sayings will help us think keenly; they will sharpen the edges of our minds. They will quicken our thoughts and enable us to understand more of life's riddles. As that occurs, the limitations of human viewpoint will slowly be replaced with the wisdom of divine perspective. The result will be a growing passion for the *active* spiritual life.

Spirituality in Action

It is quite possible that your spiritual life is limited by its narrow perspective: one-dimensional, little vision, less and less passion. That viewpoint comes from a society that sees spirituality as mostly contemplative, or at best something we do primarily for ourselves. We are learning, however, that God's Book offers a broader, deeper, richer perspective. These sayings in Proverbs have the ability to change your whole outlook. Are you willing? Before going one page further, tell the Lord that you long to have *His* viewpoint . . . that you want *His* wisdom.

∾ Maybe you are among the naïve. You have perhaps suffered the consequences of being gullible. Look again at Proverbs 1:7. Define "fear of the Lord." What does it mean when it says that such a fear is the beginning of knowledge? Growing up is a painful, slow process . . . but growth does occur. It will help you to keep a journal of the things God is teaching you these days. Start one and track your progress.

∾ Tell a friend about your interest in pursuing the active spiritual life. Explain why these sayings can be of help to you. Take along this book and read the five reasons we have the Proverbs available. Ask him (or her) to pray for you as you search for greater wisdom.

∾

2

Obedience

Wisdom shouts in the street,
She lifts her voice in the square;
At the head of the noisy streets she cries out;
At the entrance of the gates in the city, she
 utters her sayings: (1:20–21)

෴ ෴ ෴

Because I called, and you refused;
I stretched out my hand, and no one
 paid attention;
And you neglected all my counsel,
And did not want my reproof;
I will even laugh at your calamity;
I will mock when your dread comes,
When your dread comes like a storm,
And your calamity comes on like a whirlwind,
When distress and anguish come on you.
"Then they will call on me, but I will not answer;
They will seek me diligently, but they shall not
 find me, (1:24–25)

෴ ෴ ෴

So they shall eat of the fruit of their own way,
And be satiated with their own devices.
For the waywardness of the naïve shall kill them,
And the complacency of fools shall destroy
 them. (1:31–32)

❀ THE MOST IMPORTANT characteristic of the active spiritual life is obedience. But let's face it, we are a pretty wayward flock of sheep! It's not so much that we are ignorant, but rather that we are disobedient. More often than not we know what we ought to do. We just, plainly and simply, do not do it. And so our days are often spent having to endure the irksome and painful consequences of going our own way. The obedient life would help us avoid this pain, but the path of disobedience is, unfortunately, a well-worn one.

Solomon's sayings address this tendency of ours head-on. The secret of counteracting our bent toward waywardness rests with *wisdom*. In those verses you just read (Prov. 1:20–33), wisdom is personified. She is portrayed as a courageous heroine who stands in the street (symbolic of everyday life) and shouts! She is calling for our attention. She doesn't want us to drift throughout the day without taking her along as our companion. As I read these verses, I observe three facts related to wisdom:

> Wisdom is available (20–21).
> Wisdom can be ignored or spurned (24–25).
> Living without wisdom results in serious
> consequences (26–28, 31–32).

The deeper we dig into Solomon's sayings, the more clearly we discover what brings wisdom into our lives. The secret? Accepting God's reproofs and responding positively to them. Jump ahead for a moment and look at a "completive couplet" with me from Proverbs 3:11–12:

> My son, do not reject the discipline of the Lord,
> Or loathe His reproof,
> For whom the Lord loves He reproves,
> Even as a father, the son in whom he delights.

And while we're at it, look at another even more serious saying in Proverbs 29:1:

> A man who hardens his neck after much reproof
> Will suddenly be broken beyond remedy.

Reproof is from a Hebrew term that means "to correct . . . to convince." I often think of reproofs as God's proddings, those unmistakable nudges, His "still small voice." They are inner promptings designed to correct our ways. They alert us to the fact that we are off course. They communicate, in effect, "My child, that's wrong; change direction!"

These God-given "reproofs" sometimes appear in Scripture. They are spelled out—one, two, three. For example, glance at Proverbs 6:23–24:

> For the commandment is a lamp, and the teaching
>   is light;
> And reproofs for discipline are the way of life,
> To keep you from the evil woman,
> From the smooth tongue of the adulteress.

God's Book shines bright lights into dimly lit caves of immorality, shouting "Danger! Do not enter!" There are dozens of scriptures that offer similar reproofs. Such inner restraints may be silent, but they are nevertheless eloquent.

On other occasions the reproofs come verbally from those who love us. For example:

- From children: "Dad, you're sure gone a lot." Or, "Mom, you seem to be pretty impatient."

- From employers: "You're not showing the same enthusiasm you once did." Or, "You've been coming in late to work recently."

- From friends: "Is something wrong? Your attitude is negative!"

- From a wife: "I feel that you're getting pretty selfish, Hon."

- From a husband: "You don't seem very happy these days. Are you aware that your tone of voice is harsh?"

All of us have sagging character qualities that need attention. To ignore them is to open the gate that leads to disobedience. To address them is to learn and grow from God's personal reproofs. I have listed over thirty character traits in the Spirituality In Action section of this chapter, specifying some areas worth our attention.

A big question remains: Why? Why do we fail to respond to life's reproofs? What does Solomon say about the reasons we refuse reproofs? As we look back at verses 24 and 25 of chapter 1, I find four reasons reproof is refused. Hold on tight . . . they may hurt!

1   *Stubbornness.* "Because I called, and you refused. . . ."

    See that last word—*refused*? It means literally "to directly refuse." It is used most often in the Old Testament for refusing established authority, stubbornly and openly rejecting it, as in the case of Pharaoh, who refused to let the Hebrews go. In another of Solomon's sayings, the sluggard *refuses* to get a job. A stubborn will stiff-arms reproofs; a person willing to grow spiritually learns from them.

2   *Insensitivity.* ". . . I stretched out my hand, and no one paid attention."

    When Solomon states that "no one paid attention," he uses a term that suggests lack of awareness. It would correspond to the New Testament concept of being "dull of hearing." If you have ever tried to pierce through the armor plate of an insensitive individual, you know how frustrating it can be. Though wisdom "stretches out her hand," there are many who completely miss her message due to a lack of awareness. Being sensitive to others and being aware of wisdom make all the difference.

3 *Indifference.* "And you neglected all my counsel. . . ."
   To neglect means "to let go." In other words, to keep something from making any difference. This individual says, in effect, "I really couldn't care less!" This is often evidence of low self-esteem. In Proverbs 15:31–32, Solomon writes:

> He whose ear listens to the life-giving reproof
> Will dwell among the wise.
> He who neglects discipline despises himself,
> But he who listens to reproof acquires
>   understanding.

4 *Defensiveness.* " . . . and did not want my reproof."
   The Hebrew language is extremely vivid! The original word translated "did not want" means "to be unwilling, unyielding, one who won't consent." This individual is usually defensive and proud and has not learned to be open and humble.
   Obedience can override disobedience when we heed God's reproofs, which are a primary source of wisdom. It's initially more satisfying, quite frankly, to disobey. It can also seem far more exciting and adventurous. But in the long run, every time we fight against wisdom, we lose. A bit of "folk wisdom" comes to mind: "Never git in a spittin' match

with a skunk. Even if ya out-spit him, ya come out stinkin.'"

Enough said.

SPIRITUALITY IN ACTION

∾ Take a close look at these character qualities. Circle those that would rank near the top of your personal achievement list.

Alertness	Love
Appreciation	Loyalty
Compassion	Objectivity
Confidentiality	Patience
Consistency	Peacefulness
Cooperativeness	Punctuality
Courtesy	Self-control
Discernment	Sincerity
Discipline	Submissiveness
Efficiency	Tactfulness
Enthusiasm	Teachability
Flexibility	Thoroughness
Gentleness	Thoughtfulness
Honesty	Tolerance
Creativity	Sense of humor
Dependability	Sensitivity
Humility	Understanding
Initiative	Unselfishness

∾ God's reproofs don't always come directly from God's Word. He doesn't limit His warnings to specific commands or precepts found in His Book. As we discovered in this chapter, they can come through parents, friends, children, mates, employers, neighbors, a policeman, a teacher, a coach . . . any number of people. And they aren't always verbalized. A look can convey a reproof. All this week, be more sensitive to the reproofs of others.

∽ We learned of four reasons most people refuse reproofs. Can you recall them?

∽ Choose someone you know well enough to be vulnerable with and discuss which of those four reasons represents your most consistent battleground. Probe to find out why. Ask the Lord to help you break the bad habit(s) so you can get a firmer handle on how to be actively, spiritually obedient.

∼

3

Depth

My son, if you will receive my sayings,
And treasure my commandments within you,
Make your ear attentive to wisdom,
Incline your heart to understanding;
For if you cry for discernment,
Lift your voice for understanding;
If you seek her as silver,
And search for her as for hidden treasures;
Then you will discern the fear of the Lord,
And discover the knowledge of God.
For the Lord gives wisdom;
From His mouth come knowledge
    and understanding.
He stores up sound wisdom for the upright;
He is a shield to those who walk in integrity,
Guarding the paths of justice,
And He preserves the way of His godly ones.
Then you will discern righteousness and justice
And equity and every good course. (2:1–9)

✤ IN OUR IMAGE-CONSCIOUS, hurry-up lifestyle, hitting the high spots is in vogue—doing just enough to get by. No big deal . . . it's okay to ignore depth in your life so long as you project an image that says you've "got it all together."

Nonsense! People who really make a dent in society are those who peel off the veneer of shallow superficiality and live authentic lives that have real spiritual depth.

This week, let's really look at what that depth is all about. Let's allow the sayings we just read to cut cross grain against our times and speak with forceful relevance. I should warn you ahead of time, this may not be easy. Solomon takes us into a mine shaft, as it were, a place of hard work, but it will lead us to a most valuable discovery.

As I look closely at these nine verses in Proverbs 2, I find that they can be divided rather neatly into three sections:

I   The Conditions (1–4—emphasis on
the worker)
(Note: "if . . . if . . . if . . .")

II The Discovery (v. 5—emphasis on
the treasure)

III The Promises (6–9—emphasis on
the benefits)
(Note: "For . . .")

Let's dig deeper.

You say you want more depth and less superficiality? Weary of faking it? Good for you! But you must remember that breaking out of that mold is awfully hard work. Solomon writes about that when he presents the conditions of deepening our lives. "If we will do this . . . " "If we are committed to doing that. . . . " Tough talk!

I find four realms of discipline that we must come to terms with if we hope to experience the conditions of a newly-found depth in our spiritual lives.

1 *The discipline of the written Word of God.* "My son, if you will receive my sayings, / And treasure my commandments within you" (v. 1).

It is essential that we receive God's sayings—take them in on a regular basis and allow them to find lodging in our minds. Few things are more astounding in our world than biblical ignorance. People who go beneath the surface of shallow living treasure God's truths and saturate their minds with the Scriptures.

2 *The discipline of inner desire.* "Make your ear attentive to wisdom, / Incline your heart to understanding" (v. 2).

If we read that correctly, we'll need to have an
attentive ear to God's reproofs (remember last
week's subject?) and cultivate an open heart before
Him.

Are you ready for that? I mean, really motivated?
If so, look at the next level.

3 *The discipline of prevailing prayer.* "For if you cry for
discernment, / Lift your voice for understanding" (v. 3).

Perhaps the single most overlooked (and among
the most difficult) discipline in the Christian life is
consistent prayer. Prevailing prayer. Fervent prayer.
In such prayer we "cry for discernment" and we
"lift our voice for understanding." In prayer, the
sincere believer puts an end to a quick tiptoe trip
through the kingdom, chattering like children running through a mall. This person gets down to serious business.

4 *The discipline of daily consistency.* "If you seek her
as silver, / And search for her as for hidden
treasures" (v. 4).

We're talking diligence and effort here! The saying describes our seeking God's truths as though
digging for silver and searching His mind as we
would pursue hidden treasures. This is no superficial game—it's a heavy, consistent pursuit of the living God!

And the results? The discovery?

> Then you will discern the fear of the Lord,
> And discover the knowledge of God. (v. 5)

We'll find true treasure: the fear of the Lord (we'll start taking Him seriously) and the knowledge of God (we'll get to know Him intimately).

Finally, He promises us benefits—benefits from within, without, and above.

1 *From within:* wisdom, knowledge, understanding.

> For the Lord gives wisdom;
> From His mouth come knowledge and
>   understanding. (v. 6)

2 *From without:* protection.

> He stores up sound wisdom for the upright;
> He is a shield to those who walk in integrity,
> Guarding the paths of justice,
> And He preserves the way of His
>   godly one. (vv. 7–8)

3 *From above:* righteousness, justice, equity.

> Then you will discern righteousness and justice
> And equity and every good course. (v. 9)

Yes, "every good course" will accompany the path of those who seek depth.

Aren't you eager to absorb sacred things? Haven't you had your fill of superficial skating? Isn't it about time to move off the barren plateau of spiritual neutrality?

This week . . . yes, *this* week, dig in. I dare you!

Spirituality in action

∾ Memorize the first five verses of Proverbs 2. You said you wanted to grow deeper, didn't you? Well, here's a place to start. If you really want to get with it, memorize all *nine* verses.

∾ Go back and review the four disciplines taken from Proverbs 2:1–9. Be honest . . . which one represents the biggest challenge for you? Remind yourself of the discipline, pray about it, search for ways to turn your prayer into action. Think very practically:

- What are the obstacles?
- Who stands in your way?
- Why do you hesitate?
- What can be done *now*?

∾ Focus on "the fear of the Lord" and on "the knowledge of God." What do these phrases mean to you?

∾ Choose a category of your life where "the fear of the Lord" could be applied. Do the same with "the knowledge of God." Be specific. Share the results with your best friend.

4

Serenity

My son, do not forget my teaching,
But let your heart keep my commandments;
For length of days and years of life,
And peace they will add to you.
Do not let kindness and truth leave you;
Bind them around your neck,
Write them on the tablet of your heart.
So you will find favor and good repute
In the sight of God and man.
Trust in the Lord with all your heart,
And do not lean on your own understanding.
In all your ways acknowledge Him,
And He will make your paths straight. (3:1–6)

✳ THIS CHAPTER is dedicated to all of you who have worried in the past . . . all of you who are now worried . . . and all who are *making plans to worry soon!* That might sound amusing, but worry is no laughing matter. Quite frankly, it is a sin. It is, however, one of the "acceptable" sins in the Christian life. We would never smile at a Christian who staggered into his home night after night drunk and abusive. But we often smile at a Christian friend who worries. We would not joke about a brother or sister in God's family who stole someone's car, but we regularly joke about our worrying over some detail in life.

Worry is serious business. It can drain our lives of joy day after day. And there is not one of us who doesn't desire to replace it with peace of mind. In the following study we will look at Solomon's answer to this age-old habit unique to humanity.

Instead of focusing on all six verses at the beginning of Proverbs 3, let's spend some time in those last two.

They may be familiar to some, but I have the feeling they have more in them than most of us ever realized.

Please glance back and re-read the final two verses of this saying once again. As you do, think about how to add serenity to your life.

A primary rule in meaningful Bible study is to determine the context. These verses fall into a surrounding atmosphere of verses that "set the stage." Let me show you:

1:8   Hear, my son, your father's instruction . . .
1:10   My son . . .
1:15   My son . . .
2:1   My son . . .
3:1   My son . . .
3:11   My son . . .
3:21   My son . . .

Solomon is giving some wise "fatherly advice" to his son in this section of his book. If you should ever take the time to read the first seven chapters, you will discover they are intensely potent and practical. They contain vital information on how to live a stable, wise, well-balanced life. Proverbs 3:5–6, therefore, contains truth for everyday living—the kind of truth that will assist us toward a meaningful life free of worry.

Observation

There are three initial observations I want to make about Proverbs 3:5–6. Then I want to break the verses into smaller parts so that when we put the saying together it makes better sense to you.

1   There are four verbs in these two verses. Verbs are action words and therefore of special interest to all who want to live an active spiritual life.

- trust
- lean
- acknowledge
- make straight

Three of these terms are *imperatives*; in other words, they are commands. They are directed to the child of God. They are *our* responsibility: "*Trust . . . do not lean . . . acknowledge . . .*"

The last is the simple declaration of a promise. It declares God's part in the verse. It states His responsibility: "*. . . He will make your paths straight.*"

Before going to the next observation, let's understand that these four words give us a very brief outline:

I.   *My Part*
   A.   Trust!
   B.   Do not lean!
   C.   Acknowledge!
II.   *God's Part*
   A.   He will make straight. . . .

2   The same term is mentioned four times. Can you find it? Sure, it is the term *your*. Your responsibility in a given situation is to trust with all *your*

heart . . . refuse to lean on *your* understanding . . . acknowledge Him in all *your*
ways . . . so that He might make straight *your*
paths.

3   The first phrase is linked with the last phrase, giving us the main idea. The two in the middle merely
amplify the main idea. Let me explain.

  The main idea of these verses is, *I am to trust in
my Lord without reservation—with all my heart—so
that He makes my paths straight.* What is involved in
trusting with all my heart? Two actions: one negative, the other positive.

NEGATIVE: *I am not to lean on my own
          understanding.*
POSITIVE: *I am to acknowledge Him in
          all my ways.*

Clarification

Without the desire to be pedantic, I want us to dig
into the meaning of several terms. I believe it will help
you to understand their original meaning and to see
how they fit together. At the end I'll tie up all the loose
ends with an amplified paraphrase.

1   *Trust.* At the root of the original Hebrew term is the
idea of throwing oneself down, lying extended on
the ground-casting all hopes for the present and
the future upon another, finding shelter and security there.

To illustrate this, look at Proverbs 11:28:

He who trusts in his riches will fall,
But the righteous will flourish like the green leaf.

We are told *not* to trust in riches, for riches are not secure (see Proverbs 23:4–5). If you set your heart on getting rich, throwing yourself down upon them so as to find your security, you will be sadly disappointed. Riches fail and fade away. Riches do not deserve our trust.

Next, glance at Proverbs 3:21–23:

My son, let them not depart from your sight;
Keep sound wisdom and discretion,
So they will be life to your soul,
And adornment to your neck.
Then you will walk in your way securely,
And your foot will not stumble.

The word translated *securely* is the same Hebrew root word as our term trust. We are commanded by our Lord to cast ourselves *completely, fully, absolutely* on Him—and Him only!

2 *Lord.* This, as you may know, is the most intimate and sacred name for God in all the Bible. To this day Orthodox Jews will not even pronounce it. It is the title given Israel's covenant-keeping God . . . the One who is bound to His people by love and by promise. To us, it is applied to our Lord Jesus Christ, God's precious Son. We are to rely

fully upon Him, finding our safety and security in Him. He, *unlike money,* is dependable.

3   *Heart.* This does not refer to the bodily organ in the chest that pumps blood. It is used throughout the Old Testament to refer to our "inner being," that part of us that constitutes the seat of our intellect, emotion, and will—our conscience and our personality. What is the Lord saying? He is saying we are to cast upon our Savior-God our *total* trust, not holding back in any area of our mind or will or feeling. That, my friend, is quite an assignment!

4   *Understanding.* I direct your attention to this word next because it appears first in its phrase in the Hebrew Bible. Literally, the second part of verse 5 says: ". . . and upon your understanding, do not lean." This word *understanding* has reference to *human* understanding. It means that we are not to turn first to our own limited point of view, our own ideas or way of thinking, but to our Lord's wisdom.

5   *Lean.* This is the Hebrew *shan-ann,* meaning "to support oneself, as though leaning for assistance." It occurs in Judges 16:26 where blind Samson leaned against the huge pillars supporting the Philistine temple. It also appears in 2 Samuel 1:16 where King Saul leaned upon his spear for support. It represents the idea of resting one's weight upon something else as though leaning on a crutch. You will notice the strong negative: ". . . do not lean on

your own understanding."

We have a gentleman in our church who could tell you about this much better than I. He was injured on a ski outing several years ago and as a result he was confined to crutches for many long weeks. Sometimes folks would find him panting at the top of a flight of stairs. If you looked at his hands, you would notice they had gotten red and sore. The man found that leaning on crutches was *exhausting*.

So is leaning on our own understanding! If you want to spend an exhausting day, try to work out your circumstances leaning on your *human viewpoint*. Chase down all the possibilities you can think of. When you hit a dead-end street, back out, then turn down into another one. Drive fast, then slam on your brakes. Try a dash of panic, a pinch of fear, add a tablespoon of manipulation, three cups of scheming, and a handful of impatience! When you are through, consider where you have been. That is an excellent recipe for "instant depression." Furthermore, you will be mentally exhausted. Peace will flee from you.

> MAN says: *Why trust when you can worry?*
> GOD says: *Why worry when you can trust?*

6 *Acknowledge.* This means "to recognize." Rather than leaning on the manmade crutches of our own devices, we are exhorted to recognize God's presence and His will in our plight. By acknowl-

edging Him we remind ourselves that we are not alone.

7 *Make straight.* The Hebrew term means "to make smooth, straight, right." It includes the idea of removing obstacles that are in the way. It appears in a particular stem (*Piel* stem) that suggests *intensity*. In other words, when the Lord is fully relied upon to handle a given situation, He will remove all the obstacles and smooth out our path thoroughly, not halfheartedly.

Application

Now that we have analyzed all the vital parts, let's put the verses back together in an extended paraphrase:

Throw yourself completely upon the Lord—that is, cast all your present and future needs on Him who is your intimate Savior-God . . . finding in Him your security and safety. Do this with all your mind and feeling and will. In order to make this possible, you must refuse to support yourself upon the crutch of human ingenuity. Instead, recognize His presence and concern in each one of your circumstances. Then He (having taken full control of the situation) will smooth out and make straight your paths, removing each obstacle along the way.

From now on when you find yourself needing serenity and peace, turn to this paraphrase and read it aloud.

SPIRITUALITY IN ACTION

∾ Read the paraphrase I have suggested several times. But instead of reading "that is, cast *all your present and future needs* on Him," insert the specific things that you are tempted to worry about.

∾ Locate a pair of crutches. Borrow them from a friend or maybe from a local hospital. Try walking with crutches for an hour each day a week. When you are not on them, carry them in your car or prop them up by the table where you eat and by the bed where you sleep. Why? They will be a tangible, irritating reminder of how bothersome it is to the Lord for you to "support yourself on the crutch of human ingenuity."

∾ Think *seriously* about how sinful it is to worry. Yes, call it sin! Realize that it breaks that vital fellowship between you and God. Ponder the fact that when we carry our own burdens we are saying to God "No help needed!" As soon as you get even a fleeting thought to worry, deliberately give it to the Lord. Tell Him that you are refusing to lean any longer on your own abilities.

∾

5

A Sensitive Heart

My son, give attention to my words;
Incline your ear to my sayings.
Do not let them depart from your sight;
Keep them in the midst of your heart.
For they are life to those who find them,
And health to all their whole body.
Watch over your heart with all diligence,
For from it flow the springs of life. (4:20–23)

❀ AT FIRST GLANCE a sensitive heart may seem to be a rather remote area of concern for the spiritually "active" Christian. After all, what is a sensitive heart in comparison to something as active and more visible out in the real world as obedience or peace of mind? Why would anyone strive to gain and protect a sensitive heart? Well, you may be surprised. Not to be sensitive and guarded, but to unveil our hearts—putting all our secrets on display—is to open ourselves to enemy attack. Our Lord, rather, is pleased when we reserve an "inner vault" of our lives to hold His treasures. To "tell it all" is to traffic in a world of superficiality. Once we have done a little digging into this subject, I think you will realize how pertinent this piece of wisdom can be.

To begin with, let's remember what I mentioned earlier, that the *heart* in Solomon's sayings is never a reference to the organ in the chest that pumps blood. We learned in last week's reading that it is a term used to describe our whole inner being . . . the center of our mind, our emotions, and our will. In fact, the Hebrew word *labe* is used over ninety times in Proverbs alone.

So when I address "a sensitive heart," I have in mind the desirable situation of living with inner restraint, with concern for protection from the adversary, being sensitive to God's delicate leading. Now you see why I feel this is just as great a characteristic of the active spiritual life as the others we've been dealing with . . . maybe greater!

As we look at the saying of Solomon in Proverbs 4, we'll notice we are, again, in one of the "My son . . ." sections. Here is more wise counsel from a father to his family members. Observe his comment about inclining your ear to his sayings and keeping them "in the midst of your heart." Very interesting!

For the next few minutes I want us to direct our full attention to this whole idea of guarding the heart, or, as Solomon put it:

> Watch over your heart with all diligence,
> For from it flow the springs of life. (Prov. 4:23)

I notice three significant observations:

1 This is a command—"Watch over!"
2 There is an intense priority included in this command—"with all diligence."
3 The reason for the command is stated in the last part of the verse—"for. . . ."

Key Terms

As you may have noticed, there are several words that are keys toward understanding the full meaning of the statement.

Watch over, diligence, and *springs* would have to be understood before the true meaning can emerge. So, now let's dig into each one of them.

1   Rather than beginning the verse as our English version does, the Hebrew text begins with: "More than all else" or "Above all else. . . . "

    In Hebrew, when something appears first in a sentence, different from the normal word order, that word is emphatic. That means these words "more than all else" are emphatic. This tells us that our God puts a premium on the matter. Actually, these beginning words are a literal translation of "with all diligence."

    We have now established that the verse begins: "More than all else . . . "

2   The next part of the Hebrew verse refers to something that is to be watched closely. Actually, the word originally comes from a noun which means "a place of confinement." It is periodically rendered prison, and in a broader sense it means something that is closely observed, protected, preserved, or guarded.

    That gives us even more light. If we went a step further, inserting those thoughts, the verse would read: "More than all else to be closely watched and protected (as something in a confined place). . . ."

3   Now we come to the main Hebrew verb translated *watch over* in English. It is the word *nah-tzaar*, meaning "to preserve, keep." This same word occurs in Isaiah 26:3:

> "The steadfast of mind Thou *wilt keep* in
>   perfect peace,
> Because he trusts in Thee." (Emphasis mine)

The Lord's peace preserves and keeps the believer's mind, making us "steadfast." In Solomon's saying, the words "your heart" follow that same verb:

> More than all else to be closely watched and protected (as something in a confined place), preserve your heart (your inner self, the place where God speaks to you through His Word and Spirit). . . .

We are beginning to understand why this is so essential, why it is imperative for our "heart" to be watched over and preserved, kept sensitive.

4   The word *for* could just as well be rendered *because*. Now we are told *why*.

5   The Hebrew says: ". . . because from within it. . . ." Referring to the heart, the verse declares that it is to be closely protected and kept in a state of "readiness," because *within* it something extremely important occurs.

6   The Hebrew *mo-tzah* is translated "springs," but the word *source* or *direction* would be more accurate. Why is the heart to be protected and kept sensitive to the Lord? ". . . because from within it comes direction for life." Basically, then, we find this verse is dealing with the will of God—both discovering it and walking in it.

Actual Meaning

Now let's put all the pieces of our research together and see what the verse actually says. A paraphrase based on the Hebrew text might read:

> More than all else to be watched over and protected (as something in a confined place), it is imperative that you preserve and keep your heart sensitive; because from within it comes divine direction for your life.

Read that over again, this time very slowly.

The verse is saying that since your inner self—your heart—is the source and basis of knowing God's will, it is more important than *any other single thing* that your heart be in a state of readiness, receptivity, and sensitivity. Active spirituality has as its foundation a sensitive heart.

If your heart is carnal, calloused, and bent on having your own way, then direction from God for life will not come through. Look at Psalm 16:11:

> Thou wilt make known to me the path of life;
> In Thy presence is fullness of joy;
> In Thy right hand there are pleasures forever.

We learn from that statement that God wants to show His children His plan for their lives.

How God Directs

Look at Proverbs 4 for one final glance. Go back to the beginning of the chapter. In the first four verses God tells us how He directs us—how He speaks to our "heart."

First, verses 1–4:

Hear, O sons, the instruction of a father,
And give attention that you may gain
    understanding,
For I give you sound teaching;
Do not abandon my instruction.
When I was a son to my father,
Tender and the only son in the sight of my mother,
Then he taught me and said to me,
"Let your heart hold fast my words;
Keep my commandments and live."

The *Word of our Father* directs us.
Second, verses 5–7:

Acquire wisdom! Acquire understanding!
Do not forget, nor turn away from the words
    of my mouth.
Do not forsake her, and she will guard you;
Love her, and she will watch over you.
The beginning of wisdom is: Acquire wisdom;
And with all your acquiring, get understanding.

The practical application of our Father's Word to life's decisions helps direct us into His will. This explains why Solomon uses the words "wisdom" and "understanding" several times. The Lord desires for us to apply *practical common sense* in determining His will.

Third, verses 10–11, 20–22:

> Hear, my son, and accept my sayings,
> And the years of your life will be many.
> I have directed you in the way of wisdom;
> I have led you in upright paths. . . .
> My son, give attention to my words;
> Incline your ear to my sayings.
> Do not let them depart from your sight;
> Keep them in the midst of your heart.
> For they are life to those who find them,
> And health to all their whole body.

Solomon reminds us of the value of *trustworthy counselors* in these verses. Specifically, he wrote to his own child. He assures his son that the counsel of a godly parent is one of several ways God directs our hearts.

Fourth, verses 26–27:

> Watch the path of your feet,
> And all your ways will be established.
> Do not turn to the right nor to the left;
> Turn your foot from evil.

A final word regarding evaluation always helps. "Watch" means "weigh," as one would weigh baggage. Look discerningly into the matter. *Personal evaluation* (*meditation*) is another very important part of knowing God's will.

All these things explain why it is important to keep your heart open, sensitive, and carefully watched. Unless it is right before God, He cannot communicate divine direction. And unless we receive and walk in His will, misery and ultimate unhappiness are our constant companions.

Now, let me ask you: Is a "sensitive heart" really that important?

Spirituality in action

~ Let's see how well you understood Solomon's saying in Proverbs 4:23.

- "Heart" would include the_____, _____, and_____.
- "Springs" of life means _____ or _____.
- God wants to show us His will _____. True _____ False?

Check and see how you did.

~ From Proverbs 4, I presented some ways God directs us into His will:
- His Word, the Bible

- Common sense
- Trustworthy counselors
- Personal evaluation

As you look over that list, which has proven the most helpful to you? Why?

∾ Think of three ways you could do a better job of "guarding your heart." What has been allowed to slip in that could make it insensitive or slow to react? You may wish to confine your answers to three areas: My mind . . . My emotions . . . My will.

∾

6

Biblical Literacy

Then he taught me and said to me,
"Let your heart hold fast my words;
Keep my commandments and live;
Acquire wisdom! Acquire understanding!" (4:4)

∾ ∾ ∾

My son, observe the commandment of your father,
And do not forsake the teaching of your mother;
Bind them continually on your heart;
Tie around your neck.
When you walk about, they will guide you;
When you sleep, they will watch over you;
And when you awake, they will talk to you.
For the commandment is a lamp, and the
*   teaching is light;*
And reproofs for discipline are the way of life. (6:20–23)

∾ ∾ ∾

Keep my commandments and live,
And my teaching as the apple of your eye.
Bind them on your fingers;
Write them on the tablet of your heart. (7:2–3)

∾ ∾ ∾

Incline your ear and hear the words of the wise,
And apply your mind to my knowledge;
For it will be pleasant if you keep them within you,
That they may be ready on your lips. (22:17–18)

❀ FEW THINGS ARE more needed in our times than for God's people to be biblically literate. But unfortunately, even though the human mind is able to absorb an enormous amount of information, mental laziness in this important area remains a scandalous and undeniable fact.

So much for the bad news—the problem; let's focus, rather, on the good news—the solution. While there is not some quick-'n'-easy method that will suddenly get us started on the road to biblical literacy, I do believe that one particular discipline (more than any other) will get us on the right track. When I began to get serious about spiritual things, it was this discipline that helped me the most. None other has come to my rescue like this one: *memorizing Scripture.*

I can still recall more than one occasion when the memorized Word of God rescued me from sexual temptation. It was as if God drew an imaginary shade (something on the order of a Venetian blind) between the other person and me, having inscribed on the surface: "Be not deceived God is not mocked; Whatever a man sows that shall he also reap" . . . a verse I committed to memory as a young teenager. During times of great loneliness, memorized Scripture has also rescued me from the pit of depression. Verses like Isaiah 41:10 and 49:15–16, along with Psalms 27:1 and 30:5 have brought me great companionship.

Before developing that concept, let's understand that we can absorb God's Word in various ways.

First, we can *hear* it. This is the simplest, least-difficult method of learning the precepts and principles of the Bible. There are plenty of trustworthy Bible teachers and preachers in our great nation. There are churches and schools, radio and TV programs, audio and video tapes, even record albums that specialize in scriptural instruction. No one in America—except those with physical hearing impairment—has any excuse for not hearing God's Word.

Second, we can *read* it. This requires more personal involvement than simply hearing the Scriptures. Those who start getting serious about their spiritual maturity buy a copy of the Bible and begin to read it. There are numerous versions, paraphrases, and styles available. Various through-the-year Bibles can be purchased which set forth a plan that enables an individual to read through all sixty-six books of Scripture in 365 days.

Third, we can *study* it. It is at this point people begin to really mean business for God. With pen and paper, reference works, and other tools available today, the Christian starts to dig in on his (or her) own. Some take correspondence courses, others chart their own course or prefer one of the many excellent programs offered through their local church.

Fourth, we can *meditate* on it. As Scripture is heard, read, and studied, the mind becomes a reservoir of biblical truth. Those truths need to be thought through, pondered, personalized, and applied. Through times of quiet meditation, we allow the Word to seep into our cells . . . to speak to us, reprove us, warn us, comfort us. Remember those two great verses from the Book of Hebrews?

> For the word of God is living and active and sharper than any two-edged sword, and piercing as far as the division of soul and spirit, of both joints and marrow, and able to judge the thoughts and intentions of the heart. And there is no creature hidden from His sight, but all things are open and laid bare to the eyes of Him with whom we have to do. (Heb. 4:12–13)

Fifth, we can *memorize* it. What a magnificent way to replace alien and demoralizing thoughts! In all honesty, I know of no more effective way to cultivate a biblical mind and to accelerate active spirituality than this discipline.

Solomon On Scripture Memory

There are several sayings worth considering as we think of placing God's Word in our hearts.

Proverbs 4:4:

Then he taught me and said to me,
"Let your heart hold fast my words;
Keep my commandments and live."

You'll notice the words "hold fast." In the Hebrew, the words translated "hold fast" mean "to grasp, lay hold of, seize, hold firmly." It is the verb *tah-mack*; the same term is found in Isaiah 41:10, which says:

Do not fear, for I am with you;
Do not anxiously look about you, for I am your God.
I will strengthen you, surely I will help you,
Surely I will uphold you with My righteous
    right hand.

The word *uphold* is from the same verb, *tah-mack*. Scripture memory gives you a grasp, a firm grip of confidence in the Bible. As God's Word gets a grip on you, it "upholds" you!

Proverbs 6:20–23:

My son, observe the commandment of your father,
And do not forsake the teaching of your mother;
Bind them continually on your heart;
Tie them around your neck.
When you walk about, they will guide you;
When you sleep, they will watch over you;
And when you awake, they will talk to you.
For the commandment is a lamp, and the teaching
    is light;
And reproofs for discipline are the way of life.

Go back and locate "bind . . . tie." Scripture memory straps the truths of God to you. The word translated "bind" really means "to tie together, to bring something in league with something else." Our word *correlate* fits. Scriptures correlate so much better when we store them up. They help us come to terms with life; things make better sense when certain Scriptures are in place in our heads.

Proverbs 7:2–3:

Keep my commandments and live,
And my teaching as the apple of your eye.
Bind them on your fingers;
Write them on the tablet of your heart.

No clearer verses encouraging scripture memory could be found than these in The Proverbs. When we *write* something, we don't abbreviate or confuse matters. Quite the contrary, we clarify them. The Lord says "write them on the tablet of your heart." Don't be sloppy or incomplete in your memory work. It is essential that we be exact and thorough when we memorize. Without this, confidence slips away. I often think of being thorough in Scripture memory in the same way we plan a flight. Every number is precise and important (flight number, seat number, gate number) and the time as well. Being exact is extremely important!

Proverbs 22:17–18:

Incline your ear and hear the words of the wise,

And apply your mind to my knowledge;
For it will be pleasant, if you keep them within you,
That they may be ready on your lips.

I love those two sayings. They constantly encourage me to stay at this discipline! The idea of having His Word "ready on your lips" should convince us of the importance of maintaining this discipline. I say again, nothing will enhance our spiritual lives like memorizing Scripture.

Conclusion

Let's conclude with three practical suggestions that have helped me in my own Scripture-memory program.

First, it is better to learn a few verses perfectly than many poorly. Learn the place (reference) as well as the words exactly as they appear in your Bible. Do not go on to another verse until you can say everything perfectly, without a glance at the Bible.

Second, review often. There is only one major secret to memory—review. In fact, it is a greater discipline to stay current in review than to take on new verses regularly.

Third, use the verse you memorize. The purpose of Scripture memory is a practical one, not academic. Who cares if you can spout off a dozen verses on temptation if you fall victim to it on a regular basis? Use your verses in prayer, in conversations and counsel with others, in correspondence, and certainly in your teaching. Use your memorized verses with your children or mate. God will bless your life *and theirs* as you tactfully share His Word. Isaiah 55:10–11 promises:

> For as the rain and the snow come down from
>   heaven,
> And do not return there without watering the earth,
> And making it bear and sprout,
> And furnishing seed to the sower and bread
>   to the eater;
> So shall My word be which goes forth from
>   My mouth;
> It shall not return to Me empty,
> Without accomplishing what I desire,
> And without succeeding in the matter for which
>   I sent it.

Do you want to become biblically literate? Here's a good place to begin. Trust me, you will never regret the time you invest in hiding God's Word in your heart. Active spirituality demands it.

SPIRITUALITY IN ACTION

∾ Growing spiritually by becoming biblically literate will not "just happen" any more than a flat tire will automatically repair itself. It will call for extra effort! To begin realistically, select six to ten verses you have come to appreciate. Perhaps you would like to memorize several from Proverbs. Take them one at a time. Don't go on to the next until you have firmly committed the previous one to memory. And don't forget that the secret of Scripture memory is review.

∾ As situations occur in your life where the truth of what you have memorized applies, remind yourself of it. State it aloud. Use your verse(s) also in your prayers. Share them with someone else when it is appropriate. I have found that few things bring more encouragement than the repeating of Scripture when the time is right.

∾ There are Scripture-memory programs available in which you may want to enroll. One I would recommend is:

THE NAVIGATORS
POST OFFICE 6000
COLORADO SPRINGS, CO 80934

Why not write today so you can get started?

∾

7

Friendly Counsel

Deceit is in the heart of those who devise evil,
But counselors of peace have joy. (12:20)

∾ ∾ ∾

Anxiety in the heart of a man weighs it down,
But a good word makes it glad. (12:25)

∾ ∾ ∾

Even in laughter the heart may be in pain,
And the end of joy may be grief.
The backslider in heart will have his fill of his
*   own ways,*
But a good man will be satisfied with his. (14:13–14)

∾ ∾ ∾

Everyone who is proud in heart is an abomination
*   to the Lord;*
Assuredly, he will not be unpunished. (16:5)

∾ ∾ ∾

Before destruction the heart of man is haughty,
But humility goes before honor. (18:12)

∾ ∾ ∾

The foolishness of man subverts his way,
And his heart rages against the Lord. (19:3)

∾ ∾ ∾

A plan in the heart of a man is like deep water,
But a man of understanding draws it out. (20:5)

❂ EVERYONE DESIRES inner peace, but our world often creates within us a troubled heart full of anxiety and low-grade depression. Or the troubled heart may show itself in the form of inner churning, discontentment, feelings of insecurity, instability, often doubt, unrest, and uncertainty.

One answer to a troubled heart is a friend who will provide wise counsel. Friends can be used by God to provide us with a sense of peace and calm assurance that is ours to claim, if we will only open up to the wisdom of friendly counsel. Friends can provide the very best medicine for us by tuning into our troubles, listening to our words and feelings, and allowing God's Word to refresh our hearts.

Precious few of us, however, are ever aware of others' struggles. But the spiritually active Christian should work hard at learning to be more sensitive to others. The importance of this can scarcely be exaggerated. Even though you may not be deep in Bible knowledge, you should realize that you can be used effectively by God as a counselor, friend, and interested listener in the lives of others—just because you know the Lord Jesus Christ! Naturally, the deeper your knowledge of His Word, the sharper will be your discernment and the wiser will be your counsel. Job's counselors, for example, dealt him misery and spoke unwisely (you might take the time to read Job 13:3–4; 16:2; 21:34).

One of Solomon's sayings (Prov. 20:5) points out the value of a wise counselor.

> A plan in the heart of a man is like a deep water,
> But a man of understanding draws it out.

Look also at Proverbs 18:4:

> The words of a man's mouth are deep waters;
> The fountain of wisdom is a bubbling brook.

Those sayings tell us that there is within our inner beings a pool of water—often *troubled* water! Also notice that the mouth can express the troubled substance of that pool, with the help of the *man of understanding* who can lovingly draw it out so that it can be dealt with.

For example, you may feel deeply about the circumstances in which you find yourself. You cannot fully think through the depths of your feelings without the aid of one who "draws out" those feelings. And how important and comforting it is to have such people nearby!

Does that describe *you*? If so, you will be willing to take the time that is necessary to minister in this way.

Personally, I believe this is exactly what Paul has in mind when he writes: "Bear one another's burdens, and thus fulfill the law of Christ" (Gal. 6:2).

Proverbs shows us how to bear one another's burdens. Because troubled hearts wear many faces, Solomon's sayings point them out for us, along with many either stated or implied solutions. I find these six:

1   A *"counselor of peace."*

> Deceit is in the heart of those who devise evil,
> But counselors of peace have joy. (12:20)

2   A *"good word."*

> Anxiety in the heart of a man weighs it down,
> But a good word makes it glad. (12:25)

The Hebrew verb from which *anxiety* is translated, literally means "to be anxious, fearful, worried." You can detect a worried heart rather easily. It shows up on one's face.

3   A *"joyous"* heart.

> Even in laughter the heart may be in pain,
> And the end of joy may be grief. (14:13)

4   A *"good man."*

> The backslider in heart will have his fill of his own
>   ways,
> But a good man will be satisfied with his. (14:14)

5   *A humble heart.*

> Everyone who is proud in heart is an abomination
>   to the Lord;
> Assuredly, he will not be unpunished. (16:5)

> Before destruction the heart of man is haughty,
> But humility goes before honor. (18:12)

6   *A peaceful heart.*

> The foolishness of man subverts his way,
> And his heart rages against the Lord. (19:3)

Perhaps you wonder how you can detect these troubles. Look at Proverbs 20:11–12:

> It is by his deeds that a lad distinguishes himself
> If his conduct is pure and right.
> The hearing ear and the seeing eye,
> The Lord has made both of them.

The Lord says He has given you hearing ears and seeing eyes. I urge you to use *them*! Listen carefully. Watch the person with whom you speak. Be sensitive. This, of course, implies that *you* talk very little, especially during the initial contact. Now read Proverbs 16:23–24:

> The heart of the wise teaches his mouth,
> And adds persuasiveness to his lips.
> Pleasant words are a honeycomb,
> Sweet to the soul and healing to the bones.

God will be pleased to use your words as His instruments, if you allow Him to control what you say. It would be wise of you to claim the promise God gave to Moses in Exodus 4:12: "Now then go, and I, even I, will be with your mouth, and teach you what you are to say."

Who knows? You may be the one God wants to use in the life of another to bring the assurance of inner peace. This is truly spirituality in action.

SPIRITUALITY IN ACTION

∾ Now is a good time to stop, look, and listen.

Stop long enough to pray. Ask God for His wisdom to see beyond the troubled moment . . . to realize you are not alone in your troubles . . . to have a renewed sense of inner relief.

Look around. Become aware of the circle of acquaintances that is larger than your own personal world. Be sensitive. Discern opportunities for helping to avert turmoil in others . . . especially in your friends.

Listen. Instead of launching a barrage of verbal missiles, just ask a few questions, then (without offering advice) listen. Patiently and graciously hear people out. When our words are few, they become more valuable.

∾ Go back to those six examples of a troubled heart (and their solutions) from Proverbs. Which solution is *your* easiest to apply? Which the hardest? Does anybody know it? Can you say you are truly accountable? Have you given anyone permission to step into your private world? Just as others need a "counselor-friend," so do you. How about reaching out and asking someone you respect and trust to enter your secret world? Yes, you'll need to choose the person(s) carefully.

∾ Check out a reliable book on counseling from a local library or preferably your church library. Begin reading it soon. Think of ways to implement some of the techniques presented in the book. One word of caution, however: be sure that the author is committed to biblical principles and truly loves Christ as Lord. It is so important that we know a counselor's underlying faith before we embrace the concepts and techniques he (or she) espouses.

∾

8

A Controlled Tongue

The mouth of the righteous flows with wisdom,
But the perverted tongue will be cut out.
The lips of the righteous bring forth what is acceptable,
But the mouth of the wicked, what is perverted. (10:31–32)

∽ ∽ ∽

A man has joy in an apt answer,
And how delightful is a timely word! (15:23)

∽ ∽ ∽

Bright eyes gladden the heart;
Good news puts fat on the bones.
He whose ear listens to the life-giving reproof
Will dwell among the wise. (15:30–31)

∽ ∽ ∽

Pleasant words are a honeycomb,
Sweet to the soul and healing to the bones. (16:24)

∽ ∽ ∽

Like apples of gold in settings of silver
Is a word spoken in right circumstances.
Like an earring of gold and an ornament of fine gold
Is a wise reprover to a listening ear. (25:11–12)

∽ ∽ ∽

Better is open rebuke
Than love that is concealed.
Faithful are the wounds of a friend,
But deceitful are the kisses of an enemy. (27:5–6)

❀ SOLOMON'S SAYINGS HAVE a lot to say about what we say, so it must be a significant factor in our spiritual growth. In fact, "tongue," "mouth," "lips," and "words" are mentioned in Proverbs almost 150 times. That means on an average of just under five times in each of the thirty-one chapters, those words occur. Seems to me any subject mentioned that often calls for at least two chapters of our attention. Let's do that.

A key statement on the subject of the tongue is located in Proverbs 15:2, which says:

> The tongue of the wise makes knowledge acceptable,
> But the mouth of fools spouts folly.

That's one of those "contrastive couplets," isn't it? It mentions "the wise" in contrast to "fools." Interestingly, the way they use their tongues is a dead giveaway of their identity. You and I realize, of course, that the root problem is not in the mouth but in the heart—the person deep within us. Jesus taught that:

"The good man out of the good treasure of his heart
brings forth what is good; and the evil man out of the
evil treasure brings forth what is evil; for his mouth
speaks from that which fills his heart." (Luke 6:45)

Like a bucket draws water from a well, so the
tongue dips down and pours out whatever is in the
heart. If the source is clean, that is what the tongue
communicates. If it is contaminated, again, the tongue
will expose it. Let's focus on the right uses of the
tongue as we let Solomon's sayings address how the
active spirituality of a controlled tongue might demonstrate itself.

Just as we found five wrong uses, there are also five
ways the "tongue of the wise" can bring benefit to others.

1 *Wise counsel and sound advice.*

> The lips of the righteous bring forth what
>   is acceptable. (10:32)
> The lips of the wise spread knowledge. . . . (15:7)

> Without consultation, plans are frustrated,
> But with many counselors they succeed. (15:22)

> Prepare plans by consultation,
> And make war by wise guidance. (20:18)

It would also be worth your time to read and
meditate on Proverbs 25:19, 26, and 28. These three
additional sayings look at the results of listening to
unwise, unsound advice. We have all experienced

both sides of counsel—wise and unwise. How can anyone adequately measure the great benefits of wise, timely counsel?

Obviously, one without God cannot give you God's viewpoint, even though he may have beneficial words of human wisdom. We must use great discernment when seeking others' counsel. You may be surprised to read that not even the aged are always reliable:

> The abundant in years may not be wise,
> Nor may elders understand justice. (Job 32:9)

2 *Reproof, rebuke, spiritual exhortation.*

> A fool rejects his father's discipline,
> But he who regards reproof is prudent. (Prov. 15:5)

> Stern discipline is for him who forsakes the way;
> He who hates reproof will die. (15:10)

> He whose ear listens to the life-giving reproof
>   Will dwell among the wise.
> He who neglects discipline despises himself,
> But he who listens to reproof acquires
>   understanding. (15:31–32)

> Faithful are the wounds of a friend,
> But deceitful are the kisses of an enemy. (27:6)

> He who rebukes a man will afterward find
>   more favor
> Than he who flatters with the tongue. (28:23)

How rare yet how essential reproof is! Can't you think of occasions when someone wisely yet firmly rebuked you . . . and you became a better person because of it? Look again at Proverbs 27:6. I will amplify it, using a paraphrase based on the Hebrew text as a place to begin:

> Trustworthy are the bruises caused by the wounding of one who loves you; deceitful is the flattery of one who hates you.

This tells us several things:

- The one who does the rebuking should be one who loves the one he rebukes.
- The "bruise" that comes from a reproof lingers. It is not soon forgotten.
- Friendship should include the freedom to mention a criticism.
- Not all compliments come from the right motive.

So much of this matter has to do with discernment and discretion. There is the right *way* and the right *time* (not to mention the right *motive*) for such an act. God certainly is not pleased with criticism and /or rebuke from anyone and everyone at any time anyone pleases.

No finer passage of Scripture on the subject of timing our words can be found than Proverbs 25:11–12:

> Like apples of gold in settings of silver
> Is a word spoken in right circumstances.
> Like an earring of gold and an ornament
>   of fine gold
> Is a wise reprover to a listening ear.

3   *Words of encouragement.*

> A man has joy in an apt answer,
> And how delightful is a timely word! (15:23)
>
> Bright eyes gladden the heart;
> Good news puts fat on the bones. (15:30)
>
> Pleasant words are a honeycomb,
> Sweet to the soul and healing to the bones. (16:24)

By "encouragement" I mean sincere expressions of gratitude given honestly to another individual (usually in private). We so seldom do this, yet it is one of the signs of an individual practicing active spirituality.

Do you express encouragement to those closest to you? Your wife or husband? How about your children? Your teacher? Your secretary? Someone who does a quality job for you? However, we should guard against doing it *too much*. That cheapens the encouragement and makes it appear insincere. Like too large a gem on a ring, encouragement, when overdone, lacks elegance and charm.

4   *Witnessing, teaching, comforting.*

> The mouth of the righteous is a fountain
>   of life. . . . (10:11)

> The tongue of the righteous is as choice silver,
> The heart of the wicked is worth little.
> The lips of the righteous feed many,
> But fools die for lack of understanding. (10:20–21)

> The fruit of the righteous is a tree of life,
> And he who is wise wins souls. (11:30)

> The words of a man's mouth are deep waters;
> The fountain of wisdom is a bubbling brook. (18:4)

> Death and life are in the power of the tongue (18:21a)

> Deliver those who are being taken away to death,
> And those who are staggering to slaughter, O hold
>   them back.
> If you say, "See, we did not know this,"
> Does He not consider it who weighs the hearts?
> And does He not know it who keeps your soul?
> And will He not render to man according to
>   his work? (24:11–12)

Who can accurately measure the benefits gleaned from the tongue of a godly teacher, well-versed in the Scriptures? Or, how could we gauge the depth of comfort received from the lips of a close friend during a period of grief or affliction? And what about the one(s) who told you about

Christ? Remember the help you received from the gloriously good news of the Lord Jesus Christ? My, what a tremendous help!

Stop and consider this: The gospel is believed *only* when words have communicated it. The words may be written or spoken, but words are an integral part of the plan. To one who shares Christ, the tongue is essential.

Your tongue can serve no better function in life than that of faithfully, consistently communicating Christ.

5 *A good sense of humor.*

> A joyful heart makes a cheerful face,
> But when the heart is sad, the spirit is
>   broken. (15:13)
> All the days of the afflicted are bad,
> But a cheerful heart has a continual feast. (15:15)

By a sense of humor, please understand that I am *not* referring to silly, foolish talk or to distasteful, and ill-timed jesting. By humor, I mean well-chosen, properly timed expressions of wit and amusing, funny statements. I am so convinced of the value of wholesome humor, I believe one who lacks it will not be as capable a leader or as good a communicator as he (or she) could be.

There are special times when a sense of humor is needed, such as in lengthy, tense, and heated meetings, or when a serious atmosphere has settled in the home over a long period of time, or following extremely difficult experiences in our lives.

How quickly and how easily we forget to laugh! And yet, how healthy laughter is. Look at that last phrase of the final saying I quoted above. The Hebrew text literally says that the cheerful heart *"causes good healing."*

How do you measure up, my friend? Honestly now, have you become so serious you can no longer enjoy yourself (and others)? Let's face it, if there is one, general criticism we Christians must accept without argument, it is that we have become altogether too serious about everything in life. We exclude or ignore most every opportunity for a good, healthy laugh! We're "uptight," far too intense, and much too critical of ourselves and others. As a result, our tolerance and understanding are extremely limited. May God loosen us up! And may He ultimately enable us to grow spirituality from cultivating a more controlled tongue.

SPIRITUALITY IN ACTION

∾ Turn to the New Testament in your Bible and read James 3:1–12 slowly and aloud. Do that *at least three times.* After each reading, sit quietly and talk with the Lord about how much you want Him to gain full control over your tongue.

∾ Think of two ways you could use your tongue in a more helpful manner. How about implementing both?

∾ A final suggestion *must* deal with improving your sense of humor. In all honesty, have you become rather testy? Maybe a bit too tedious, even negative? Perhaps it is due to too many hours at work. Burnout always robs us of our humor (workaholics don't have a good sense of humor). It may stem from your serious temperament or your circumstances. Enough of that! Take a few extra hours off this weekend. Deliberately focus on the brighter side of life. Select a humorous book to read or a comedy on television or a light-hearted film at the movies . . . and let your hair down! People who cultivate a healthy sense of humor give themselves permission to enjoy life. Start there.

∾

9

Contentment

Better is a dish of vegetables where love is,
Than a fattened ox and hatred with it. (15:17)

∾　∾　∾

Better is a little with righteousness
Than great income with injustice. (16:8)

∾　∾　∾

Better is a dry morsel and quietness with it
Than a house full of feasting with strife. (17:1)

❀ WHEN WAS THE last time you met someone who was truly content and at peace with the world? There are many such people! They usually got the wisdom to be that way by learning from the experiences of an active spiritual life. They discovered a sense of inner peace and contentment through their walk with God. But many folks eat their hearts out, suffering from the contagious "If Only" disease. Its germs infect every slice of life.

If only I had more money
If only I could make better grades
If only we owned a nicer home
If only we hadn't made that bad investment
If only I hadn't come from such a bad background
If only she would have stayed married to me
If only our pastor were a stronger preacher
If only my child were able to walk
If only we could have children
If only we didn't have children

If only the business could have succeeded
If only my husband hadn't died so young
If only I would've said "No" to drugs
If only they had given me a break
If only I hadn't had that accident
If only we could get back on our feet
If only he would ask me out
If only people would accept me as I am
If only my folks hadn't divorced
If only I had more friends

The list is endless. Woven through the fabric of all those words is an attitude that comes from the simple choice to see the negative side of life, the choice to be unhappy about almost everything that happens. Taken far enough, it leads to the dead-end street of self-pity—one of the most distasteful and inexcusable of all attitudes. Contentment, on the other hand, comes from another one of those simple choices, one that doesn't allow ourselves or others to listen to our list of woes. We simply choose to create a different kind of list—a positive one—for if we don't, people won't stay around us very long. Discontented souls soon become lonely souls.

I am so pleased that Solomon did not overlook these choices involving contentment. On three separate occasions he wrote sayings for all of us to read, especially when we are tempted to feel sorry for ourselves. You may have already noticed that all three are "comparative couplets" where the

former things named are "better than" the latter. For
example:

> Better is a dish of vegetables where love is,
> Than a fattened ox and hatred with it. (15:17)

Who needs a T-bone steak? So what's the big deal
about chateaubriand for two if it must be eaten in an
absence of love? Several years ago I smiled as I read
about a gal at a cocktail party trying to look happy. A
friend noticed the huge sparkling rock on her finger
and gushed, "My! What a gorgeous diamond!"

"Yes," she admitted, "it's a Callahan diamond. It
comes with the Callahan curse."

"The Callahan curse?" asked her friend. "What's
that?"

"Mr. Callahan," she sighed.

Solomon asks, "What good is it to have more and
more of anything if hatred is part of the package?"

Here's another eloquent rebuke:

> Better is a dry morsel and quietness with it
> Than a house full of feasting with strife. (17:1)

Quietness or strife, our choice is obvious—if we listen to the voice of wisdom. For many people, a simple
bowl of oatmeal served in a tranquil setting is far better than partying with constant coming and going,
endless activity and loads of food . . . but strife.

> Better is a little with righteousness
> Than great income with injustice. (16:8)

Can't miss the point of that one either. Spiritual truths often show up as the opposite of what we would normally (humanly) expect. Here, "little" is better than "great." Remember the meaningful slogan of environmental sustainability, "small is beautiful"? Or remember the seeming opposites in Christ's Sermon on the Mount? The meek shall inherit the earth (Matt. 5:5). The poor in spirit are blessed (Matt. 5:3). Just "a little" with righteousness outstrips the Taj Mahal with injustice.

The rich *and* the poor must hear this. Those who want (and have) much and those who feel they need more are equally in need of this counsel. Contentment rarely has anything to do with one's financial status. Poor people can be content; rich people can be discontent. The choices we make and the objectives we have are what breed contentment or discontentment. Wisdom does not produce greed. Greed is cancer of the attitude, not caused by insufficient funds but poor choices. Contentment comes when we desire peace; discontentment comes when we heard its subtle whisper of more . . . more . . . more . . . more . . . "

Look at the words of 1 Timothy 6:6–10, 17–19 very carefully, as if you are reading them for the first time:

> But godliness actually is a means of great gain, when accompanied by contentment. For we have brought nothing into the world, so we cannot take anything out of it either. And if we have food and covering, with these we shall be content. But those who want to get

rich fall into temptation and a snare and many foolish and harmful desires which plunge men into ruin and destruction. For the love of money is a root of all sorts of evil, and some by longing for it have wandered away from the faith, and pierced themselves with many a pang. . . .

Instruct those who are rich in this present world not to be conceited or to fix their hope on the uncertainty of riches, but on God, who richly supplies us with all things to enjoy. Instruct them to do good, to be rich in good works, to be generous and ready to share, storing up for themselves the treasure of a good foundation for the future, so that they may take hold of that which is life indeed.

As the Chinese philosopher Lao-Tzu once said:

There is no calamity greater than lavish desires. There is no greater guilt than discontentment. And there is no greater disaster than greed.

SPIRITUALITY IN ACTION

∾ As you read through that "if only" list, try to re-phrase each of them into a positive statement of contentment. Which ones were the hardest for you to rephrase?

∾ Now go back and read those words from the Chinese philosopher. How do they apply? In what way can you say you are willing to address your secret longing? And while we're at it, is there ever a proper place for being discontented? Explain your answer, especially in light of the words "if we have food and covering . . . be content."

∾ Jesus, on more than a few occasions, spoke directly to the issue of always wanting more. In His immortal Sermon on the Mount, He stated "You cannot serve God and mammon" (Matt. 6:24). What is the difference between "earning" and "serving" money? One more thought: If Jesus were to live on earth today, where do you think He would be employed? What kind of car would He drive? How much money would He earn? Do you think He would periodically fly first class? Would He ever feel a slight sting of discontentment? Why? Or why not?

∾

10

Resisting Temptation

For the commandment is a lamp, and the
    teaching is light;
And reproofs for discipline are the way of life,
To keep you from the evil woman,
From the smooth tongue of the adulteress.
Do not desire her beauty in your heart,
Nor let her catch you with her eyelids.
For on account of a harlot one is reduced
    to a loaf of bread,
And an adulteress hunts for the precious life.
Can a man take fire in his bosom,
And his clothes not be burned?
Or can a man walk on hot coals,
And his feet not be scorched?
So is the one who goes in to his neighbor's wife;
Whoever touches her will not go
    unpunished. (6:23–29)

ω   ω   ω

The one who commits adultery with a woman
    is lacking sense;
He who would destroy himself does it.
Wounds and disgrace he will find,
And his reproach will not be blotted out. (6:32–33)

✤ Solomon shoots straight. I find that rather refreshing in our day of gray definitions and bold rationalizations. The sayings you just read are timeless and no less relevant today than they were when the ink was still wet. The ways to resist temptation are obvious, but there is always the opportunity to fall . . . the snares to trip us up. Whether it's in the area of fortune, fame, power, or pleasure—the opportunities to resist lust present a constant pressure on our souls. Many there are who give in; but many there are who choose to resist. Those who have victory in this area will find a valuable asset in their quest for active spirituality.

Let me remind you that these words and warnings appear in another of the "My son" accounts. As a father, Solomon wanted to leave trustworthy counsel for his son to read and heed. Perhaps he wrote these words with an extra amount of passion since his own father David had suffered the consequence of yielding to lustful temptations many years earlier. Though David's adultery happened before Solomon's birth, no one can doubt that he was ever aware of the consequences that came in the wake of the king's compromise. Solomon was reared in a context that never let him forget his father's moral failure.

Solomon asserts the standard of Holy Scripture:

> For the commandment is a lamp, and the
>   teaching is light;
> And reproofs for discipline are the way of life. (6:23)

That is always a place to find one's standard—God's perfect and Holy Word. Not the media. Not others' opinions. Not the books written by fellow strugglers. Not even our own conscience, which can be seared, calloused, or prejudiced. The "lamp" of God's precepts, the "light" of His teaching—*these* provide us with unfailing direction. Furthermore, as we learned earlier, His reproofs goad us into line and intensify our discipline.

So then, what do we learn from Solomon's sayings when we want to resist the lure of a lustful lifestyle? How do we triumph over this kind of temptation?

1   Stay away from "the evil woman" (or man).
2   Guard against the "smooth tongue" that invites you in.
3   Refuse to entertain secret desires of the opposite sex's beauty.
4   Don't let those alluring eyes captivate you.

Now, wait just a minute! *Why* would Solomon take such a hard stand on resisting lust's appeal? Without the slightest hesitation, he sets forth the truth, which so few stop to think through today. As we read these sayings, we find several specific reasons for resisting:

First, the adulteress "hunts for the precious life." When the list is discovered, the backwash for the adulterer is undeniable. To name only a few of the consequences:

Loss of character	Injury to his career
Loss of self-respect	Smearing of his name
Loss of others' respect	Embarrassment to his church
Loss of his family	Draining of his finances
Loss of his testimony	Possibility of disease
Loss of his joy and peace	Beginning of deceitfulness and secrecy

Second, the hot fire of punishment will begin and never be fully extinguished. Burn scars are among the most obvious and painful. The one who yields to lustful temptations "will not go unpunished."

Third, yielding to temptation reveals a "lack of sense"; a self-destructive process is begun.

Fourth, "wounds and disgrace" will never be fully erased. Let that word *never* make its full impact.

Solomon isn't through!

He goes even further, describing in lurid detail how lust initially appears so appealing, so accepting, so safe . . . yet in the end, it is like "an arrow" and "a snare."

> At the window of my house I looked out through the lattice. I saw among the simple, I noticed among the young men, a youth who lacked judgment. He was going down the street near her corner, walking along in the direction of her house at twilight, as the day was fading, as the dark of night set in.

> Then out came a woman to meet him, dressed like a prostitute and with crafty intent. (She is loud and defiant, her feet never stay at home; now in the street, now in the squares, at every corner she lurks.) She took hold of him and kissed him and with a brazen face she said: "I have peace offerings at home; today I fulfilled my vows. So I came out to meet you; I looked for you and have found you! I have covered my bed with colored linens from Egypt. I have perfumed my bed with myrrh, aloes and cinnamon. Come, let's drink deep of love till morning; let's enjoy ourselves with love! My husband is not at home; he has gone on a long journey. He took his purse filled with money and will not be home till full moon."

> With persuasive words she led him astray; she seduced him with her smooth talk. All at once he followed her like an ox going to the slaughter, like a deer stepping into a noose till an arrow pierces his liver, like a bird darting into a snare, little knowing it will cost him his life. (Prov. 7:6–23, NIV)

Wake up! Let the truth be heard, my friend. When the escapade ends, gross consequences follow . . . and *they* never end.

This is a day when many are becoming soft on those who fall morally, when the idea of abstinance has to be sold and justified. At the risk of overkill, let me ask you: Do you find Solomon soft? Stop and meditate on the final six words in the scripture you just read: " . . . it will cost him his life." I call that about as severe a consequence as one can imagine.

Talk about the active side of spirituality! Now is the time to come to terms with temptation. It may not fully go away, but resisting each instance is a simple matter of choice. Choosing life rather than disgrace and punishment is really not all that difficult.

SPIRITUALITY IN ACTION

∾ Because Solomon shoots straight, I see no reason to back off and trade diplomacy for truth. A good place to start is with a few pointed questions:

- Are you flirting with lust or resisting it? Do you encourage sexual come-ons?
- Have you worked out a plan for lust to keep a foot in the door? Be painfully honest.
- Is there some secret sin you are harboring? Someone you're meeting with? Magazines? Video cas-

settes? How about those hotel late-night TV movies? Or cable television channels?

I plead with you; run for your life from those flames of temptation. If you don't, they are sure to grow hotter as the months pass and you will get burned. To add insult to injury, your quest for spiritual maturity will come to a grinding halt. Remember, burn scars last a lifetime.

∾ You may be dangerously close to sexual fire. It could be so close that you find yourself unable to back off. It may call for professional help. *Get it.* Contact a pastor for reference if you don't know whom to see . . . or call someone you respect and start back toward purity. Let me urge you, also, to burn whatever you have hidden away—make a *clean* sweep of it! Tell your illicit partner it is over. Do that even if you don't feel like doing it. Act now.

∾ I have already mentioned the importance of being accountable. Once again, I must affirm how valuable it would be for you to allow another trusted individual (or two) into the secret chambers of your life. In order for this to happen, you need to be the one who makes the first move. Even if you don't have a major battle in this area, you *still need a point of accountability.* An accountability group forms a safety net. A few trusted friends who love you too much to let you exist in a self-made world of secret struggles and personal blind spots can become your best insurance investment. Resisting lustful temptations will require team effort. Start building your team!

~

11

Diligence

Go to the ant, O sluggard,
Observe her ways and be wise,
Which, having no chief, officer or ruler,
Prepares her food in the summer,
And gathers her provision in the harvest.
How long will you lie down, O sluggard?
When will you arise from your sleep? (6:6–10)

❧ ❧ ❧

The soul of the sluggard craves and gets nothing,
But the soul of the diligent is made fat. (13:4)

❧ ❧ ❧

Commit your works to the Lord,
And your plans will be established. (16:3)

❧ ❧ ❧

The mind of man plans his way,
But the Lord directs his steps. (16:9)

❧ ❧ ❧

Do not love sleep, lest you become poor;
Open your eyes, and you will be satisfied
    with food. (20:13)

❧ ❧ ❧

The plans of the diligent lead surely to advantage,
But everyone who is hasty comes surely
    to poverty. (21:5)

❀ DILIGENCE AND industry are qualities that make projects successful, yet we all have a tendency to procrastinate.

> *Pro·cras·ti·nate* To put off intentionally and habitually, postpone . . . to put off . . . reprehensibly the doing of something that should be done.
> —Webster's Seventh New Collegiate Dictionary

Thanks, Webster.

Not that we needed a definition, but sometimes it helps to nail things down. When we procrastinate, we deliberately say "later" but usually think "never." It's the manana syndrome: "Someday, we gotta get organized." Which, being interpreted, is really saying, "Who cares if it *ever* gets done?" People who procrastinate have no definite plans to accomplish the objective. They simply push it into the slimy ooze of indefiniteness, that murky swamp where the thought of good intentions slips in over its head.

Do you need to learn more diligence? Do you really want to put *feet* to your active spirituality? Then Solomon's sayings to the rescue!

First off, Solomon assures us that we have all the mental equipment we need to do the deed.

> The plans of the heart belong to man,
> But the answer of the tongue is from the Lord. (16:1)

That ability to plan is unique to mankind. "Orderly thinking" (16:1, MLB) is ours and ours alone. We have a built-in capacity to think things through . . . to plan things out. Horses don't. Rabbits can't. Chickens won't. But you and I can *and should*.

Second, Solomon affirms we can also have the *desire* to get the thing done.

> Commit your works to the Lord,
> And your plans will be established. (16:3)

We even have divine assistance available. But please don't kid yourself; this is not automatic. A desire doesn't guarantee accomplishment. I recall another saying of Solomon:

> The soul of the sluggard craves and gets nothing,
> But the soul of the diligent is made fat. (13:4)

Deep within our beings rest rival foes: Sluggard vs. Diligence. The fight is on. Both have desires, you understand. Even Sluggard "craves," but he accomplishes zilch. He doesn't follow through. He postpones: "Maybe someday."

But Diligence?

The plans of the diligent lead surely to advantage,
But everyone who is hasty comes surely to
poverty. (21:5)

Then why don't we always overrule Sluggard and
give the nod to Diligence? Why do we opt for procras-
tination more often than not? I have thought about
that a lot (even while sitting here, realizing I needed to
get at it). Here are my conclusions:

- Either we set goals that were unwise or unrealistic
- Or we attempted to do something that was not
  God's will
- Or we allowed Sluggard to win when he arm-
  wrestled Diligence!

So? Surprisingly, Solomon says we need to take a
trip out to an anthill. In fact, God *commands* us to
do so!

Go to the ant, O sluggard,
Observe her ways and be wise,
Which, having no chief, officer or ruler,
Prepares her food in the summer,
And gathers her provision in the harvest.
How long will you lie down, O sluggard?
When will you arise from your sleep? (6:6–10)

Ouch! I find it more than a little humiliating to
think of standing six feet above a tiny insect and being
told to bend down and learn from its ways. But what

lessons the ant teaches us! Those tiny pedagogues model several valuable messages:

- They don't need some superintendent over them.
- They get the essentials done first.
- They work ahead of time so they can relax later.
- They do it all without fanfare or applause.

What happens if we fail to follow the ant's example?

- We continue to procrastinate.
- We begin to resemble "a vagabond."
- We ultimately become dependent on others.

Furthermore, we miss one of life's most delightful rewards, which Solomon describes in these words:

Hope deferred makes the heart sick,
But desire fulfilled is a tree of life. . . .
Desire realized is sweet to the soul. (Prov. 13:12, 19)

Our hearts get "sick" when we keep putting our hope on hold. What is it that is so "sweet to the soul"? Accomplishment. For example:

- A garage cleaned spic and span.
- The storm windows attached before winter's first blast.
- Those twenty pounds gone from our bodies.
- The whole yard mowed . . . and trimmed.
- The room addition finished (yes, that includes paint!).
- A car waxed.

- A new dress made.
- Pictures labeled and placed in the photo album.
- The chapter written!

Spirituality in action

꙳ Take the Scriptures literally. Go out to the closest anthill and watch. Watch very carefully. If you look closely you will see those tiny creatures handling a load much larger and heavier than their own bodies. Furthermore, you'll see none of them kicking back, arguing with each other, or procrastinating. Diligent creatures, those ants.

꙳ Perhaps what keeps most of us from getting a big job done is one of two things:

- Getting started
- Spelling out a plan

Think about both for a few moments. Why not plunge in right away? Better still, how about writing down a procedure. Organize the workload—you know the age-old motto: Plan your work, then work your plan. That's not very clever or creative, but it is still effective.

꙳ Fill in the blanks:

- I need to finish

  _____

- What keeps me from it is

_____

_____

and

_____

- By_____ (time) on _____ (date), I
  will complete that project.

When you do, reward yourself! Your "realized desire" deserves loud applause.

≈

12

Submission to Sovereignty

The fear of the Lord is the beginning of wisdom,
And the knowledge of the Holy One
 is understanding.
For by me your days will be multiplied,
And years of life will be added to you. (9:10–11)

ॐ ॐ ॐ

The Lord will not allow the righteous to hunger,
But He will thrust aside the craving of
 the wicked. (10:3)

ॐ ॐ ॐ

The way of the Lord is a stronghold to the upright,
But ruin to the workers of iniquity. (10:29)

ॐ ॐ ॐ

When a man's ways are pleasing to the Lord,
He makes even his enemies to be at peace
 with him. (16:7)

ॐ ॐ ॐ

Many are the plans in a man's heart,
But the counsel of the Lord, it will stand. (19:21)

ॐ ॐ ॐ

The king's heart is like channels of water in the
 hand of the Lord;
He turns it wherever He wishes. (21:1)

❊ AT FIRST GLANCE the list of sayings on the previous page may appear more like a hodgepodge of random thoughts. A closer look, however, reveals a common theme—one we tend to forget or ignore. It is the theme of God's almighty sovereignty.

Now you may be asking what the sovereignty of God has to do with active spirituality. Well, plenty, as we shall soon see.

Since our generation is so hung up on human ingenuity and carnal cleverness, we tend to give people strokes that only God deserves.

- A battle is won . . . we hang medals on veterans.
- A degree is earned . . . we applaud the graduates.
- A sum of money is donated . . . we engrave contributors' names in bronze.
- An organization stays in the black through hard times . . . we give the CEO a bonus.

- A writer or scientist makes an outstanding contribution . . . we award the Pulitzer or Nobel prize.
- A sermon meets numerous needs . . . we thank the preacher.

There's nothing at all wrong with showing appreciation, just so we acknowledge the One who really deserves the maximum credit and give Him the greatest glory. But since He works out His will so silently (and often mysteriously), we feel a little spooky saying much about His almighty sovereignty.

Too bad. More needs to be said these days about God's sovereignty. Why? Because when so little is being said, man starts to strut his stuff. As you begin to develop some of the characteristics of the spiritually active Christian, you will be tempted to take more and more of the credit for your spiritual growth. Don't! Pride will destroy you. Humility is the one essential ingredient you can never be without. Look back at those timeless sayings from Solomon's pen. Read them slower this time.

Do you see what they are saying? God is in charge. Actually He is the unseen stronghold to the upright and the unseen obstacle in the way of the wicked (10:3, 29). He is so powerful that He can honor those who please Him by changing the attitudes of those who once felt enmity toward His followers (16:7). And get this: Once it is all said and done, after our plans have been hammered out, thought through, reworked, decided on, and distributed—it is ultimately His counsel that will stand.

That doesn't make you nervous, does it? You're not bothered by these comments about a doctrine that has become controversial, are you? Solomon didn't learn of God's sovereignty from John Calvin, remember; Calvin learned it from Scripture. Relax, this isn't simply "reformed doctrine," it is revelational doctrine. Frankly, I find it extremely comforting and enormously relieving. But for many (especially the hard-charging, do-it-yourself types) submission to sovereignty, even in the spiritual realm, is irksome. That's too bad.

Let's dig a little deeper into Proverbs 21:1:

> The king's heart is like channels of water in the hand
>   of the Lord;
> He turns it wherever He wishes.

Immediately we can see it is a "comparative couplet" (see earlier discussion in chapter 1). Something is compared to something else. Most comparative couplets end with the comparison and leave it at that. But this saying comes to a conclusion in what could be called the declarative part of the proverb . . . leaving the reader a timeless principle.

Observe the comparison: "The king's heart is like channels of water in the hand of the Lord." The Hebrew sentence doesn't begin with "the king's heart" but rather with "like channels." The Hebrew term translated *channels* is one that refers to small irrigation ditches that run from a main source—a reservoir—out into dry thirsty flatlands needing a cool drink. In other words: "Like irrigation canals carrying water is the heart of the king in Jehovah's hand. . . ."

What's the point? The king's heart (his inner being), the internal part of him that makes decisions, breathes out and communicates attitudes and policies, edicts and laws. . . is actually in the Lord's hand. As a result, he may appear to be in charge, but the entire matter from start to finish silently and sovereignly rests with the Lord. So it is with your spirituality. A yielded, submissive spirit is the most effective way to appropriate God's power in your life. The sovereign Lord, not the king or an*y other* monarch or leader, qualifies to be the *u.c. with u.a.*—Ultimate Chief with Ultimate Authority.

How can anyone say such a thing, especially if the human authority is an unbeliever? Well, just finish reading Solomon's saying: "He (the Lord Himself) turns it wherever He wishes." Literally, He "causes it to be bent wherever He is pleased." God is calling the shots. Again, I ask you—Do you have struggles with that? If so, then you will really churn over this:

> But at the end of that period I, Nebuchadnezzar,
> raised my eyes toward heaven, and my reason re-
> turned to me, and I blessed the Most High and
> praised and honored Him who lives forever;
> For His dominion is an everlasting dominion,

And His kingdom endures from generation to
generation.
And all the inhabitants of the earth are accounted
as nothing,
But He does according to His will in the host of
heaven
And among the inhabitants of earth;
And no one can ward off His hand
Or say to Him, 'What hast Thou done?'" (Dan. 4:34–35)

Those are the words of a powerful king who was describing how God had worked him over prior to his coming full circle.

What is true of ancient kings is also true of modern bosses. Your boss. Or anyone else who thinks he is in full control. Yes, even you. God is ultimately going to have His way. You may decide to wrestle or attempt to resist, but I've got news for you; He's never met His match. He will win. He will have His way.

And just in case today is a high-level stress day when submitting to your sovereign Lord doesn't seem all that fair or fulfilling, take my advice: Do it anyway. You'll be glad later. Maybe sooner.

SPIRITUALITY IN ACTION

∾ Do some digging on your own. Find a couple or three reliable reference works and write out your own expanded definition of God's sovereignty.

∾ Pick out two Bible characters whose lives were uniquely directed by God. Read up on both. *Joseph* is a beautiful example from the Old Testament. (Genesis 50:15–21 is a classic reference.) And from the New Testament, *Saul of Tarsus* is another worth examining. (Note especially Acts 9:1–20.) God's hand on Joseph's life illustrates how He can change a heart from resentment to forgiveness. His hand on Saul's life illustrates His sovereign ability to bring a proud, strong-willed type to his knees in utter humility.

∾ Get alone. Find a quiet place where you can think. And pray. And reorder your life. Speak openly and audibly to the Lord and tell Him of your willingness to "lay down your arms." Acknowledge your stubborn streak. Express your desire to let Him have His way. Invite Him to take charge of each segment of your life. Yes, each one.

∾

13

Industriousness

The hand of the diligent will rule,
But the slack hand will be put to forced labor. (12:24)

∾ ∾ ∾

A slothful man does not roast his prey,
But the precious possession of a man is diligence. (12:27)

∾ ∾ ∾

The soul of the sluggard craves and gets nothing,
But the soul of the diligent is made fat. (13:4)

∾ ∾ ∾

Laziness casts into a deep sleep,
And an idle man will suffer hunger. (19:15)

∾ ∾ ∾

The sluggard says, "There is a lion outside;
I shall be slain in the streets!" (22:13)

∾ ∾ ∾

The sluggard says, "There is a lion in the road!
A lion is in the open square!"
As the door turns on its hinges,
So does the sluggard on his bed.
The sluggard buries his hand in the dish;
He is weary of bringing it to his mouth again.
The sluggard is wiser in his own eyes
Than seven men who can give a discreet
    answer. (26:13–16)

✿ MANKIND BENEFITS from work and industriousness. They are what has enabled us to create great civilizations. Many people, however, live under the false impression that work is a curse. Many others dream of being free from having to work. Some even attempt to quote Scripture to verify their position that work was the sad consequence of Adam's fall in the Garden of Eden. Wrong!

Before sin ever entered the human race—while total innocence prevailed—Adam was assigned the task of cultivating the Garden (Gen. 2:15). Work is not a curse. The curse that followed the Fall had to do with the hassles—the thorn- and thistle-like irritations that now accompany one's work—not work itself. Work, alone, is a privilege, a challenge to indolence, an answer to boredom, and a place to invest one's energy . . . not to mention to provide for our physical needs. And make no mistake about it, active spirituality takes work.

Throughout the Bible we are encouraged to be industrious, to be people of diligence, committed to the tasks in life that need to be accomplished. Some, however, do not consider this a privilege, but a drag. For those folks, the idea that spiritual growth is hard is an attractive option. Therefore, let's snap on our zoom lens and focus on this practical reality.

Of all the Scriptures that address the issue of laziness, none are more eloquent than the sayings of Solomon. Among the terms he uses for the lazy, "sluggard" seems to be his favorite. When I trace my way through the Proverbs, I find no less than six *characteristics* of the sluggard.

1   *The sluggard has trouble getting started:*

> How long will you lie down, O sluggard?
> When will you arise from your sleep?
> 'A little sleep, a little slumber,
> A little folding of the hands to rest'—
> And your poverty will come in like a vagabond,
> And your need like an armed man. (6:9–11)

You may remember that in chapter twelve we discussed the active spirituality of diligence, so there is no need to repeat what was presented in that study. Nevertheless, there is no getting around it: laziness focuses on the obstacles, the excuses that loom large on the front end of a task. Those who are lazy just can't seem to roll up their sleeves and plunge in full bore.

2   *The sluggard is restless:* He (or she) may have desires, but the trouble comes in implementing them:

> The soul of the sluggard craves and gets nothing,
> But the soul of the diligent is made fat. (13:4)

> The desire of the sluggard puts him to death,
> For his hands refuse to work;
> All day long he is craving,
> While the righteous gives and does not hold
>   back. (21:25–26)

It is not uncommon for the lazy to be extremely skilled, creative people. They can talk and dream and even sketch out the game plan, but the discipline of pursuit is lacking. As we just read, the "craving" goes on "all day long," but little gets accomplished. When it comes to the sluggard's getting off dead center and getting the job done, forget it.

3   *The sluggard takes a costly toll on others:*

> He also who is slack in his work
> Is brother to him who destroys. (18:9)

That last word, "destroys," pulsates with liabilities. A lazy employee doesn't simply hold an organization back, he *destroys* its motivation and drive. A lazy player doesn't just weaken the team, he *destroys* its spirit and diminishes its will to win. A lazy pastor doesn't merely limit a church, he *destroys* its enthusiasm, its passion to win souls and meet needs. Before long, everyone must do more to compensate for the sluggard's negative influence.

4 *The sluggard is usually defensive:*

> The sluggard is wiser in his own eyes
> Than seven men who can give a discreet
>   answer. (26:16)

Can't you just hear it . . . all those rationalizing comments? Unfortunately, it is this clever ability to cover up or explain away that keeps the lazy person from coming to terms with reality.

5 *The sluggard is a quitter:*

> A slothful man does not roast his prey,
> But the precious possession of a man is
>   diligence. (12:27)

In this saying, there is the telltale mark of laziness: an absence of thoroughness.

- He likes to catch fish, but not to clean them.
- He loves to eat, but don't expect him to help with the dishes.
- He can add a room onto the house, but getting it painted is another story.

He'd rather sleep than work; he'd rather focus on why something can't be helped . . . then blame the government for not caring (see Prov. 19:15).

6 *The sluggard lives by excuses:*

> The sluggard says, 'There is a lion outside;
> I shall be slain in the streets!' (22:13)

That saying always makes me smile. Those lions in the street are nothing more than a fertile imagination gone to seed. The "lion" returns. . . . The sluggard says, "There is a lion in the road!

> A lion is in the open square!"
> As the door turns on its hinges,
> So does the sluggard on his bed.
> The sluggard buries his hand in the dish;
> He is weary of bringing it to his mouth
>   again. (26:13–15)

If it weren't so tragic, the analogy of a sluggard on a bed resembling a door on a hinge would be hilarious!

On the road to active spirituality, no one ever automatically or instantaneously overcame laziness. If you desire to be more industrious, today is the best day to start a new direction. The best place to start is by admitting it if you are lazy . . . Stop covering it up. I dare you!

A young fellow rushed into a gas station to use the pay phone. The manager overheard his telephone conversation as he asked:

"Sir, could you use a hardworking, honest young man to work for you?" (pause) "Oh . . . you've already got a hardworking, honest young man? Well, thanks anyway!"

The boy hung up the phone with a smile. Humming to himself, he began to walk away, obviously happy.

"How can you be so cheery?" asked the eavesdropping service-station manager. "I thought the man you talked to already had someone and didn't want to hire you."

The young fellow answered, "Well, you see I *am* the hardworking young man. I was just checking up on my job!"

If you called your boss, disguised your voice, and asked about *your* job, what do you think would be the boss's answer?

Or think about this. What if you could "ring up" God, disguise yourself, and ask him what *He* thought of your diligence in pursuing the active spiritual life. What do you think He would say?

SPIRITUALITY IN ACTION

∾ Go back over that list of six characteristics. Spend enough time on each to see yourself mirrored in the scene. Which two represent your greatest area(s) of weakness? Write them down.

∾ Now that you have identified a couple of weaknesses in your work style, spell out a game plan for correcting those areas where you have a tendency to be lazy. Be specific, practical, and realistic. Begin your strategy with such words as: "Today, I will begin to . . ." or "From now on, I am going to . . ."

∾ Do you happen to have a spiritually lazy acquaintance who holds you back from an active Christian walk? Frequently, an unhealthy or unwholesome association will give us just the excuse we need to settle for less than God's best for us. Do you really need to spend that much time with him (or her)? If you do, be honest enough to address the problem head-on. Ask the person either to join you in a strategy for growth or to step aside so you can. Maintaining industriousness in our commitment to active spirituality occasionally requires us to confront someone holding us back by using those familiar words, "Lead, follow . . . or get out of the way!"

∼

14

Balance

If you are slack in the day of distress,
Your strength is limited. (24:10)

❧   ❧   ❧

Two things I asked of Thee,
Do not refuse me before I die:
Keep deception and lies far from me,
Give me neither poverty nor riches;
Feed me with the food that is my portion,
Lest I be full and deny Thee and say,
   "Who is the Lord?"
Or lest I be in want and steal,
And profane the name of my God. (30:7–9)

✺ THE LONGER I live the more I realize the ease with which we can slip into extremes and the harm that can do to our spiritual lives. I see it all around me and sometimes, to my own embarrassment, I find it in myself. A major prayer of mine as I grow older is, "Lord, keep me balanced!"

- We need a balance between work and play (too much of either is unhealthy and distasteful).
- We need a balance between time alone and time with others (too much of either takes a toll on us).
- We need a balance between independence and dependence (either one, all alone, leads to problems).
- We need a balance between kindness and firmness, between waiting and praying, resisting and cooperating,
between saving and spending,
between taking in and giving out,
between wanting too much and expecting too little,

between warm acceptance and keen discernment, between grace and truth.

For many folks, the struggle to keep things in balance is not an annual conflict, but more like a daily struggle.

Solomon mentions one such struggle: adversity.

If you are slack in the day of distress,
Your strength is limited. (Prov. 24:10)

When things are adverse, life gets simple; survival becomes our primary goal. Adversity is a test on our resiliency, our creativity. Up against it, we reach down deep into our inner character and we "gut it out." We hold up through the crisis by tapping into our reservoir of inner strength.

But another far more subtle struggle is the opposite extreme: prosperity—when success smiles and things begin to come easily, when there's plenty of money, when everybody applauds, when we get all our ducks in a row and the gravy starts pouring in, watch out! *That's* the time to hang tough. Why? Because, in times of prosperity, things get complicated. Spiritual goals get cloudy. Integrity is on the block. Humility is put to the test. Consistency is under the gun. Of the two struggles, I'm convinced that prosperity is a much greater test than adversity. It is far more deceptive.

The one who wrote the following sayings understood all this much better than we. Listen to his wise counsel, actually a prayer:

Two things I asked of Thee,
Do not refuse me before I die:
Keep deception and lies far from me,
Give me neither poverty nor riches;
Feed me with the food that is my portion,
Lest I be full and deny Thee and say, "Who
    is the Lord?"
Or lest I be in want and steal,
And profane the name of my God. (30:7–9)

The man had lived enough years and had seen enough scenes to boil his petition down to two specifics:

- Keep me from deceiving and lying.
- Give me neither too little nor too much.

It is that second request that intrigues us, isn't it? That is the one he amplifies. Why does he resist having too little? There would be the temptation to steal. Whoever doubts that has never looked into the faces of his own starving children. At that moment, feeding them could easily overrule upholding some high-and-mighty principle. Adversity can tempt us to profane the name of our God.

And why does he fear possessing too much? Ah, there's the sneaky one! It's *then*—when we're fat-'n'-sassy—that we are tempted to yawn at spiritual things, take credit for our success, and think heretical thoughts like, "God? Aw, who really needs Him?" Prosperity can tempt us to presume on the grace of our God.

So we need balance. The adversary of our souls is the *expert* of extremes. He never runs out of ways to push us to the limit . . . to get us so far out on one end, we start looking freaky and sounding fanatical as we cast perspective to the winds.

The longer I live, the more I must fight the tendency to go to extremes . . . and the more I value balance.

SPIRITUALITY IN ACTION

∾ Let's do a little honest appraisal, okay? To help keep your appraisal on a fairly reliable footing, two things will be needed:

- Your calendar
- Your checkbook

Looking through your *calendar*, do you find a balance or imbalance? Too many things going on or too little time with others? And while you're looking, when was the last time you got away for an overnight . . . just to be refreshed? Is your time being kept in balance?

Next, go back over the last several months in your checkbook. Go ahead, take a look! Do your expenditures reflect balance or imbalance? Too much (or not enough) on yourself? How about God's part? Is the way you spend your money an indication of balance?

∾ Adversity or prosperity . . . toward which extreme

are you? How are you handling the pressures? Does anyone know—I mean someone who can really pray you through these testy waters? Try not to underplay or overreact to the challenge. You would be wise to memorize Proverbs 30:7–9 this week.

∾ Let me put it straight: Is Christ truly Lord? The future of your spiritual pilgrimage depends on your answer. Being the Bulwark of Balance, Jesus is eminently capable of escorting you through life's challenges, including this one. It may be essential (you decide) for you to set aside one hour this week and turn all the details of your life over to Him, including your calendar and your checkbook.

∾

15

Acceptance

Wisdom shouts in the street,
She lifts her voice in the square;
At the head of the noisy streets she cries out;
At the entrance of the gates in the city, she
    utters her sayings;
"How long, O naïve ones, will you love simplicity?
And scoffers delight themselves in scoffing,
And fools hate knowledge?" (1:20–22)

∽ ∽ ∽

"Because they hated knowledge,
And did not choose the fear of the Lord.
They would not accept my counsel,
They spurned all my reproof.
So they shall eat of the fruit of their own way,
And be satiated with their own devices.
For the waywardness of the naïve shall kill them,
And the complacency of fools shall
    destroy them." (1:29–32)

❀ By ACCEPTANCE, I am not referring to external acceptance from others, but to internal acceptance within one's self. I'm not talking about our encounters with someone or something else that influence our efforts. What I have in mind is how we personally accept or welcome the things of God—His leading, His tests, His reproofs, His will, His wisdom. Some people are so given to internal resistance that they regularly fail to learn the lessons Truth attempts to teach. While others spurn His ways, many glean God's message and follow His principles. The person wholeheartedly engaged in active spirituality desires to be in that latter category.

As a pastor, I have been amazed at the difference among Christians when it comes to acceptance of instruction. Some never seem to learn. While there are always those who are sensitive and open to spiritual things—in fact, a few can't seem to get enough!—there are those who are exposed to the same truths year after year, but they fail to soak in. Not until I came across three types of individuals in the sayings of Scripture did I understand why. All three have two things in common—they are people of opposition, but they oppose in different ways and they even develop a passion for active spirituality.

The Simple

The "simple" are called "naïve ones" by Solomon. The Hebrew *pah-thah* means "to be spacious, wide." In noun form it is frequently translated "door, entrance." It is the idea of being completely open, believing every word, easily misled, even enticed . . . an easy prey to deception. The naïve are susceptible to evil and wide open to any opinion. They are usually inadequate when it comes to coping with life's complexities, especially if it requires a great deal of spiritual or mental discipline.

Reading through Proverbs, I find that the simple:

* are insensitive to danger or evil:

> For at the window of my house
> I looked out through my lattice,
> And I saw among the naïve,
> I discerned among the youths,
> A young man lacking sense,
> Passing through the street near her corner;
> And he takes the way to her house,
> In the twilight, in the evening,
> In the middle of the night and in the darkness. (7:6–9)

Suddenly he follows her,
As an ox goes to the slaughter. . . . (7:22a)

- do not envision the consequences:

  "Whoever is naïve, let him turn in here,"
  And to him who lacks understanding she says,
  "Stolen water is sweet;
  And bread eaten in secret is pleasant."
  But he does not know that the dead are there,
  That her guests are in the depths of Sheol. (9:16–18)

- are gullible . . . they lack caution:

  The naïve believes everything,
  But the prudent man considers his steps. (14:15)

- fail to learn . . . they plunge in again and again!

  The prudent sees the evil and hides himself,
  But the naïve go on, and are punished for it. (22:3)

The Scoffer

Here is a person quite different from the simple. The scoffer "delights in his scoffing." The Hebrew term *lootz* means "to turn aside, to mock." It is the thought of rejecting with vigorous contempt . . . to refuse and to show disdain or disgust for spiritual truth.

Our response is to "whip 'em into shape," to apply a lot of intense discipline so they will stop scoffing. More than likely, that's wasted effort. Solomon reminds us:

He who corrects a scoffer gets dishonor for himself.
And he who reproves a wicked man gets insults for
  himself.

Do not reprove a scoffer, lest he hate you,
Reprove a wise man, and he will love you. (9:7–8)

This explains why all these fall under the general heading of "the opposition", not "the accepting." The scoffer won't listen to words of correction. He vigorously opposes it.

A wise son accepts his father's discipline,
But a scoffer does not listen to rebuke. (13:1)

Nor will he (or she) appreciate our attempts to bring about a change.

A scoffer does not love one who reproves him,
He will not go to the wise. (15:12)

The Fool

The Hebrew root term for fool is *kah-sal,* meaning "to be stupid, dull." Its Arabic counterpart means "to be sluggish, thick, coarse." Don't misunderstand. The fool has the capacity to reason, he just reasons wrongly. Fools are absolutely convinced of one thing: they can get along quite well *without* God. Scripture reserves some of its severest rebukes for fools, but also notice the presence of the desirable kind of person in the same couplet:

- Fools traffic in wickedness . . . They play with it.

    Doing wickedness is like sport to a fool;
    And so is wisdom to a man of understanding. (10:23)

- Fools place folly on display . . . They flaunt it.

Every prudent man acts with knowledge,
But a fool displays folly. (13:16)

- Fools arrogantly "let it all hang out."

  A wise man is cautious and turns away from evil,
  But a fool is arrogant and careless. (14:16)

Strong words! Nevertheless, they need to be heard. They also help explain why acceptance is so desirable. To be more accepting is not only real to some and common among humanity in general, but it may also be *your* personal challenge. If so, it's time to come to terms with it. And that is necessary even if you already have some little areas of acceptance in only a few quiet corners of your heart. You need more. Few things please our Lord more, or characterize active spirituality better, than a teachable spirit.

Do you possess one?

SPIRITUALITY IN ACTION

∾ See if you can, in your own words, define the opposite of the three types of individuals we found mentioned in the sayings of Scripture; try to dig deeper than just "the wise". This "new" list will be a good description of the "spiritually accepting" person.

- The simple

- The scoffer

- The fool

Can you think of a biblical example of each type and its opposite?

∾ Which type of individual represents an area of challenge for you? Can you call to mind a recent occasion that illustrates this fact? If you have children, can you see this same trait being played out in one (or more) of them? Spend some time thinking how you can help counteract or nurture that tendency.

∾ Since no one else (according to Proverbs) seems that effective when it comes to changing the simple, the scoffer, or the fool, the responsibility for doing so rests with the individuals themselves. What are some things you can *do* personally to turn the tide? Aside from wishing and praying, describe two or three action steps that will begin to move you toward the ranks of acceptance. When do you plan to start?

∾

16

Forgiveness

He who mocks the poor reproaches his Maker;
He who rejoices at calamity will not go
    unpunished. (17:5)

∾ ∾ ∾

Do not rejoice when your enemy falls,
And do not let your heart be glad when he stumbles;
Lest the Lord see it and be displeased,
And He turn away His anger from him.
Do not fret yourself because of evildoers,
Or be envious of the wicked;
For there will be no future for the evil man;
The lamp of the wicked will be
    put out. (24:17–20)

∾ ∾ ∾

If your enemy is hungry, give him food to eat;
And if he is thirsty, give him water to drink;
For you will heap burning coals on his head,
And the Lord will reward you. (25:21–22)

❀ HAVE YOU SPENT much time around someone who's life is characterized by a spirit of forgiveness? It is a beautiful thing to witness. Contrast this with the person who is eaten up with the cancer of revenge. These folks are walking time bombs. Festering bitterness searches for and usually finds ways to explode. Often, those who suffer the brunt of another's revenge are innocent bystanders. They just happen to be in the way when the volcano erupts. Clearly, a choice between forgiveness or revenge is a major challenge we all face at one time or another.

I think Sir Francis Bacon had the right idea when he wrote:

> Revenge is a kind of wild justice; which the more man's nature runs to, the more ought law to weed it out. . . . certainly, in taking revenge, a man is but even with his enemy; but in passing over it, he is superior, for it is a prince's part to pardon.

Is it possible that you would like to replace revengeful thoughts and acts with those of kindness and forgiveness? If so, you are on the right road to active spirituality. There won't be a better time to expose revenge in all its ugliness. Like a tumor that will ultimately turn a healthy body into a corpse if it is ignored, this disease-carrying growth must be removed. The sooner, the better.

But how? Here's where God's Word comes to our rescue! First, we must do something that is painful within ourselves—we must forgive our enemy; and second, we must do something that is profitable for our "enemy"—we must show kindness.

Forgive Your Enemy

First things first. The revenge clings tenaciously within us because we have not forgiven the other person. Sounds simple—too simple—doesn't it? How do I know I've not forgiven someone else? I rejoice at the thought of calamity striking him or her . . . but Solomon's saying declares that such an attitude "will not go unpunished." The stinging acid of resentment will eat away at my own inner peace. Furthermore, by our rejoicing when our enemy falls, we somehow hold back God's anger (Prov. 24:17–18). In some mysterious way, the Lord's taking vengeance on our behalf is connected to our releasing all of that to Him. By our refusing to forgive, revealed in our looking with delight on the offender's calamity, we hinder the divine process.

Vengeance is God's work, but it awaits our releasing it to Him.

> Vengeance is Mine, and retribution,
> In due time their foot will slip;
> For the day of their calamity is near,
> And the impending things are hastening upon them.
> For the Lord will vindicate His people,
> And will have compassion on His servants;
> When He sees that their strength is gone,
> And there is none remaining, bond or free."
> (Deut. 32:35–36)

Because that is true, all thought of our taking revenge must be released. When we do, we "leave room (or give a place) for the wrath of God" (Rom. 12:19) to go to work. Read the following slowly and very carefully:

> Never pay back evil for evil to anyone. Respect what is right in the sight of all men. If possible, so far as it depends on you, be at peace with all men. Never take your own revenge, beloved, but leave room for the wrath of God, for it is written, "Vengeance is Mine, I will repay, says the Lord." (Rom. 12:17–19)

So much for the first part: forgive, forgive, forgive!

Show Kindness Toward Your Enemy

Now then, the second step proves the validity of our forgiveness . . . we do something beneficial on behalf of the one we once resented.

If your enemy is hungry, give him food to eat;
And if he is thirsty, give him water to drink;
For you will heap burning coals on his head,
And the Lord will reward you. (Prov. 25:21–22)

- Your now-forgiven enemy is hungry? Provide a nice meal.
- Your now-forgiven enemy is thirsty? Prepare a cool drink.

"That's easy enough," you say. "But what does all this mean about heaping burning coals on his head?"

In ancient days, homes were heated and meals were fixed on a small portable stove, somewhat like our outside barbecue grills. Frequently, a person would run low on hot coals and would need to replenish his supply. The container was commonly carried on the head. So as the individual passed beneath second-story windows, thoughtful people who had extra hot coals in their possession would reach out of the window and place them in the container atop his head. Thanks to the thoughtful generosity of a few folks, he would arrive at the site with a pile of burning coals on his head and a ready-made fire for cooking and keeping warm. "Heaping burning coals on someone's head" came to be a popular expression for a spontaneous and courteous act one person would voluntarily do for another.

The saying was still popular in the New Testament era, since Paul referred to it in a context very similar to the ones we've been considering in the sayings of Solomon.

"But if your enemy is hungry, feed him, and if he is thirsty, give him a drink; for in so doing you will heap burning coals upon his head." Do not be overcome by evil, but overcome evil with good. (Rom. 12:20–21)

I find it interesting that the only two places in Scripture where this custom is mentioned are in identical settings: demonstrating kindness toward someone who was once an offender—an enemy. A tough assignment? Certainly. But worth some serious thought by the spiritually active Christian? Absolutely.

Equally significant is Paul's concluding remark. Instead of being "overcome by evil" (that's what happens when the cancer of revenge continues to spread its tentacles), we are told to "overcome evil with good."

Revenge will continue to siphon our peace, our joy, and our love until we forgive—and I mean *completely* forgive—and ultimately prove our forgiveness through acts of kindness, courtesy, and thoughtfulness.

SPIRITUALITY IN ACTION

∾ Do you have someone's face on the dart board of your mind? Be honest, now . . . 'fess up! Have you been entertaining thoughts of revenge toward another individual? Do you smile with cruel cynicism when you read the popular bumper sticker: "I don't get mad . . . I get even." If so, confession is the first step toward cleansing and renewing spiritual growth in this area of your life. Are you willing to admit to yourself and to the Lord that you've looked forward to the day when calamity would strike that person?

∾ This is the time to work through whatever it takes to get rid of your secret and to practice forgiveness and kindness. Again, I repeat, the ugly tumor of revenge *must* come out. If you can't seem to handle the surgical procedure alone, call for help. A minister, a priest, a counselor, a friend, a family member, a teacher—somebody who will not only hear you but help you. You'll need to talk it through (remember Proverbs 20:5 which we considered in chapter seven) and hammer out a plan to find peace within. Call on the Lord for His help. Take your time. Do a thorough job of cleaning all the corruption out of the wound. Don't be surprised if tears flow. That's not only acceptable; it's advantageous.

∾ Begin to think of a way to "heap burning coals" on the head of that person. It may be in the form of a kind letter you write. Perhaps you could put in a good word for him (or her). Or send a gift—something tangible. Don't fake it. If you cannot pull it off with a pure motive, wait. The time will come when you will have an opportunity to do so.

17

Affirmation

Do not envy a man of violence,
And do not choose any of his ways.
For the crooked man is an abomination to the Lord;
But He is intimate with the upright. (3:31–32)

~ ~ ~

For jealousy (envy) enrages a man,
And he will not spare in the day of vengeance.
He will not accept any ransom,
Nor will he be content though you give
     many gifts. (6:34–35)

~ ~ ~

A tranquil heart is life to the body,
But passion (envy) is rottenness to the bones. (14:30)

~ ~ ~

Do not let your heart envy sinners,
But live in the fear of the Lord always.
Surely there is a future,
And your hope will not be cut off.
Listen, my son, and be wise,
And direct your heart in the way. (23:17–19)

~ ~ ~

Do not be envious of evil men,
Nor desire to be with them;
For their minds devise violence,
And their lips talk of trouble. (24:1–2)

❀ ENVY IS ONE OF the great enemies of active spirituality. It keeps us from loving our neighbors, from functioning with others in a community, and from affirming people's unique worth. Envy steals contentment from the heart. Petrarch was so right when he wrote:

> Five great enemies to peace inhabit within us: avarice, ambition, envy, anger, and pride. If those enemies were to be banished, we should infallibly enjoy perpetual peace.

Envy is the desire to equal another in achievement or excellence or possessions. It comes from a desire to have what we lack, rather than to give what we have. The ancients referred to it as a malignant or hostile feeling. Augustine lists it among "the passions (that) rage like tyrants and throw into confusion the whole soul . . . with storms from every quarter." He then describes such a soul as having an "eagerness to win what was not possessed. . . . Wherever he turns, avarice can confine him, self-indulgence dissipate him, ambition master him, pride puff him up, envy torture him, sloth drug him. . . ."[1]

An apt term: *torture*. Such is the toll envy takes on its victims. A *tortured* person will find active spirituality a tough task indeed.

Jealousy and *envy* are often used interchangeably, but there is a slight difference. Jealousy begins with full hands but is frightened or threatened by the loss of its plenty. It is the resistance to losing what one has, in spite of the struggle to keep it. Envy is not quite the same. Envy begins with empty hands, mourning what it *doesn't* have. In *Purgatorio*, Dante portrays it as "a blind beggar whose eyelids are sewn shut." One who is envious is unreasonable because he is sewn up within himself.

Such torture can scarcely be exaggerated. Jealousy wants to possess what it already has; envy wants to have what another possesses.

Interestingly, both emerge in Scripture from the same Hebrew term *qua-nah*, which means "to be intensely red." It is descriptive of one whose face is flushed as a sudden surge of blood announces the rush of emotion. To demonstrate the grim irony of language, *zeal* and *ardor* and *envy* all come from a common linguistic root. The same emotion that "enrages a man" (Prov. 6:34) also floods him with zeal to defend his country or adore his wife and family.

On several occasions the sayings of Scripture include warnings against our being consumed by envy.

As you read earlier, we are not to envy one who is violent, or to choose any of his ways. An abrupt burst of anger may get quick results, but in the long run, the long-term consequences far outweigh the initial benefits (Prov. 3:31–32). In fact, the cultivation of envy brings "rottenness to the bones" (Prov. 14:30).

I find it extremely significant that the most-often repeated warnings regarding envy have to do with our being envious of the sinner, of evil men and their wayward lifestyle (Prov. 23:17; 24:1). That should not surprise us. The active spiritual person must avoid the favorite unguarded mind game so many folks play in imagining how stimulating it would be to live it up . . . to throw restraint to the winds and "let it all hang out." Face it, sin has its sensual and seasonal pleasures. They may be short-lived and passing (Heb. 11:25), but they're certainly not dull and boring!

Furthermore, the wicked appear to get away with murder. Haven't you noticed? They maneuver their way through life with relative ease, they get out of trouble by lying and cheating, they can own and drive whatever, live wherever, and con whomever they wish out of whatever they want. And it seems as though they usually get away with it! And all this without accountability or responsibility. If something gets to be a hassle, bail out of it! If somebody gets in the way, walk over him! When we compare that self-satisfying lifestyle to the disciplines of spirituality and the restraints of righteousness, it doesn't take an advanced degree from Dartmouth to see how envy can creep in.

And while we're at it, envy isn't limited to inner tortures over the ungodly. Spiritually active people can be just as envious of their fellow Christians. It happens so quickly! That age-old, red-face flush can happen in dozens of life's scenes:

- When we hear a more polished speaker
- When we watch a more capable leader
- When we visit a bigger church
- When we read a better book
- When we meet a more beautiful, thinner woman (or a more handsome or charming man)
- When we observe a more effective evangelist
- When we ride in a more luxurious car
- When we listen to a more popular singer

The envy-list has no end. Not even preachers are immune!

Envy can be even better understood—and conquered—by looking at its opposite, affirmation. Look again at the list above. Does it take that much energy to admire the more polished speaker, perhaps learn from him, but accept him for what he is and ourself for what we are? You might have qualities that the polished speaker lacks. If you both were in the same group your individual qualities might complement each other. That's how communities and families function successfully. Everyone plays a different role. You and the speaker are both different—and unique—in the eyes of God. Why not affirm and glory in the diversity of God's creation? Why not be grateful that we all aren't alike, that we all aren't polished speakers? How boring that would be!

Another helpful perspective on envy and affirmation is the fact that we live in a very competitive society. Talking with people from less competitive cultures is a marvelous way to get a handle on envy. It allows us to gain the inner peace that comes when we accept others without comparing ourselves with them.

Perhaps affirmation and toleration are the antidotes you need. It is possible that as you age, you will "mellow out" and learn to appreciate the fact that we all have strengths and limitations. There was once a time, perhaps when you were younger, when you felt you could do anything, but reality intervened.

The reality of truth allows you to push envy aside. The fact is . . . you won't be able to have or own or enjoy some of the things you see and hear others enjoying. So be it. There is no sense in torturing yourself; finding peace is much more important. Be happy for the other person whom God has blessed; be grateful and affirming that they have realized some of their dreams—just as you have.

Now is the time to triumph over envy. How much more peaceful to be contented with our lot! How much better to "rejoice with those who rejoice"! A mark of spiritual maturity is the ability to appreciate another more gifted than we . . . to applaud another more honored than we . . . to enjoy another more blessed than we. Such a wholesome attitude of affirmation underscores our confidence in and allegiance to the sovereignty of God, who "puts down one and exalts another" (Ps. 75:7).

As spiritually active Christians, let's expose our inner struggle with envy to the Physician of our souls. Like revenge, envy is another tumor we dare not ignore. Let's invite the Physician's scalpel and allow Him to excise it. Join me as we, together, open our hearts to affirmation.

SPIRITUALITY IN ACTION

ᔕ Before the week ends, get a Bible concordance and look up every reference in Scripture under the headings of "envy" and "envious." Read each verse you locate slowly and aloud. Look for antidotes to envy. Let the Spirit touch your inner spirit with the full impact of His truth. It may hurt, but it will ultimately help bring healing and spiritual growth.

ᔕ Do a little analysis of *your* battle with envy and of your reluctance to be more tolerant and accepting. Does it spring most often from a comparison of material possessions? *Why?* Does it increase when you are around more educated or capable people? *Why?* Does it emerge when you think of "what might have been" in your own life? *Why?* Could it be that envy is at the root of your underlying critical spirit? Could this explain why you have become more suspicious of those whom God has chosen to bless? Since "jealousy is as severe as the grave"

(Song of Solomon 8:6), it can leave its victim immobilized. Talk to God about this.

∾ This weekend, take a little extra time to turn your attention from others' achievements and blessings to your own. This is a valuable spiritual exercise. Count your blessings one by one. Make a mental list of what the Lord has done *for* you and *through* you. Don't miss your years of service, your health, your own touch on others' lives, or your continued ability to be of help to a few specific individuals. Pray for contentment. Pray for healing from the plague of comparison. Pray for a grateful spirit. Pray for spiritual growth from this process. Finally, be big enough to pray for at least three other people who are being used by God in a greater or broader way than He has chosen to use you. Accept them for what they are; accept yourself for what you are. (You might even write an affirming letter of encouragement to those people.) Pray for your mutual success, your continued effectiveness, and your protection from enemy attacks.

∾

18

Tolerance

A man's discretion makes him slow to anger,
And it is his glory to overlook a transgression. (19:11)

~ ~ ~

Deliver those who are being taken away to death,
And those who are staggering to slaughter, O hold them
  back.
If you say, "See, we did not know this,"
Does He not consider it who weighs the hearts?
And does He not know it who keeps your soul?
And will He not render to man according to his work?
  (24:11–12)

~ ~ ~

To show partiality is not good,
Because for a piece of bread a man will transgress. (28:21)

~ ~ ~

The righteous is concerned for the rights of the poor,
The wicked does not understand such concern. (29:7)

~ ~ ~

There is a kind of man whose teeth are like swords,
And his jaw teeth like knives,
To devour the afflicted from the earth,
And the needy from among men. (30:14)

✿ TOLERANCE PROVIDES "wobble room" for those who can't seem to measure up. It also allows needed growing room for the young and the restless. It smiles rather than frowns on the struggling. Instead of rigidly pointing to the rules and rehearsing the failures of the fallen, it stoops and reaches out, offering fresh hope and humble understanding.

Intolerance is the antithesis of all that I have just described. Unwilling to "overlook a transgression" (Prov. 19:11), it tightens the strings on guilt and verbalizes a lot of shoulds and musts. It frowns as it piles more shame on an already shame–satiated soul. Unwilling to overlook differences, it sets up one's self as the standard. The heart of the intolerant has not been broken, not really. For many, it has become unbreakable, judgmental, without compassion—and very shallow.

Don't misunderstand; most of this lack of tolerance is not overt, but subtle. You can detect it in a look; it is not usually spoken. To draw upon Solomon's saying, instead of delivering those who are going under, those "staggering to slaughter," the intolerant excuse their lack of assistance by saying, "We did not know this" (Prov. 24:11–12). But the Lord knows better. The Lord is well aware of how much active spirituality needs to exhibit impartiality in its dealings with others.

Is more tolerance something you would like to gain? Be honest; do you have difficulty leaving room for differing opinions? Are you impatient with others who can't measure up? Could it be that you have tasted for so long the ecstasies of conquest that you've forgotten the agonies of defeat? I can think of any number of ways, however, where tolerance can demonstrate an active spiritual life.

- The healthy can be patient with the sickly.
- The strong have no trouble adapting to the weak.
- The fleet do well with the slow.
- The thin and physically fit refuse to judge those who struggle with their weight.
- The productive have understanding of the drudge.
- The wealthy can really imagine the pain of being poor.
- The quick minds know quite a lot of the embarrassment of being a slow learner.
- The coordinated accept the awkward.
- The pragmatic listens to the philosophical.
- The engineer respects and tries to learn from the artist.

- The stable and secure work on understanding the fragile and fearful.

Karl Menninger wrote with keen perception:

> When a trout rising to a fly gets hooked on a line and finds himself unable to swim about freely, he begins with a fight which results in struggles and splashes and sometimes an escape. Often, of course, the situation is too tough for him.

> In the same way the human being struggles with his environment and with the hooks that catch him. Sometimes he masters his difficulties; sometimes they are too much for him. His struggles are all that the world sees and it naturally misunderstands them. It is hard for a free fish to understand what is happening to a hooked one.[2]

Perhaps you fall into the category of a "free fish." Having never felt the sting of a hook or the choking panic of being caught, tolerance will help you keep your pride in check! Solomon muses over certain kinds of people who are "pure in their own eyes," whose "eyelids are raised in arrogance." Interestingly, their teeth become swordlike, sharp as knives. And whom do they devour, according to the saying of Scripture? "The afflicted . . . the needy" (Prov. 30:14). Why, of course! The intolerant invariably choose to devour those they consider "beneath them."

This is an excellent time to bring even the slightest intolerance that may be lurking in your life out in the open and place it before the Lord. Take a look at Psalm 139, especially the last two verses. Note David's petition: "Search me, O God . . . And see if there be any hurtful way in me, / And lead me in the everlasting way." What a perfect occasion to talk with the Lord about your desire to become more tolerant.

Before closing off our study, let's consider one more saying worth our examination:

The generous man will be prosperous,
And he who waters will himself be watered.
(Prov. 11:25)

True, the initial interpretation of Solomon's words is related to being generous with one's money, but broaden it to include being generous of spirit—broad-shouldered and big-hearted. Such an individual will not be restrictive in spirit or demanding, but "generous" of soul. The good news is that the same will come back to him. Others, in turn, will be accepting and tolerant. What a marvelous picture of active spirituality at work!

It may be hard for a free fish to understand what is happening to a hooked one, but it isn't completely impossible. Our Lord knew no sin, did no sin, had no sin. Although He was never "hooked," His heart went out to those who were ashamed of their sin. On one occasion He had the audacity to stand in defense of a woman caught in the very act of adultery.

Remember His words of tolerance bathed so beautifully in grace? After shaming those self-appointed judges who were ready to stone her, He looked deeply into the fallen woman's eyes and gently reassured her, "Neither do I condemn you; go your way; from now on sin no more" (John 8:11). Not a hint of intolerance.

If more tolerance is what you need, it is imperative that you go for it. I'm thinking not only of you, but of others who might suffer if you don't. Those around you will be relieved by your humility and will be encouraged to know that you are striving for greater tolerance in your life. It's a virtuous pursuit: becoming easy to live with.

SPIRITUALITY IN ACTION

∾ Do your best to describe the contrast between tolerance and intolerance. Two clarifications need to be thought through:

- When does tolerance become wholesale permission? How far is too far?

- There must be times when intolerance is appropriate, since Jesus drove the moneychangers out of the temple. Name another time or two in Scripture when our Lord refused to give ground. What does that imply?

∾ Is there someone you know who could use an arm around a shoulder, a word of encouragement, and a few hours of companionship? Perhaps this person didn't measure up to the expectations of you or

others, or holds to a different opinion on a controversial subject, or recently went through a time of
personal disappointment that took the wind out of
his or her sails. Would you risk making contact?
Reach out and demonstrate compassion on that
person's behalf. Listen to where he or she is coming
from. *Really* listen. Call to mind Solomon's counsel regarding our being slow to anger: "It is his glory
to overlook a transgression" (Prov. 19:11). The active spiritual Christian is often allowed to witness
such genuine healing.

∾ Finally, it is time for some reflection. Since it is true
that intolerance and arrogance are often related,
could it be that you have forgotten those occasions
when you blew it . . . when you were like that trout,
hooked and unable to get free? For the next ten
minutes, vividly recall the pain of feeling alone,
ashamed, and misunderstood. Think of a person or
two who laid aside all pride as he (or she) invested
time and demonstrated compassion. Ask the Lord
to give you the courage to do the same. Time may
be more of the essence than you realize.

∾

19

Taking Responsibility

Four things are small on the earth,
But they are exceedingly wise:
The ants are not a strong folk,
But they prepare their food in the summer;
The badgers are not mighty folk,
Yet they make their houses in the rocks;
The locusts have no king,
Yet all of them go out in ranks;
The lizard you may grasp with the hands,
Yet it is in kings' palaces. (30:24–28)

❀ ANTS, BADGERS, locusts, and lizards . . . sounds like roll call for Noah's Ark! Or an advertisement for a new jungle movie. But no, these four creatures are discussed in Proverbs 30:24–28—another of those amazing sayings from Scripture that speaks volumes to us today.

According to the opening statement in verse 24, each of these four creatures is "small on the earth, but . . . exceedingly wise." Each represents a contrast. We shouldn't think that size means insignificance. Within each is a remarkable ability . . . and, likewise, a hidden peril. As we shall see, each teaches a lesson on taking responsibility we would do well to learn.

The Ant

We have already looked at the ant earlier, so there's no need to linger here over details already discussed. Suffice it to say that without some higher-ranking authority to drive them on, without great strength (one human foot can stomp several of them into oblivion!), the ant nevertheless works, works, works.

The Badgers

This creature isn't big either, but it is extremely independent. A member of the weasel family, badgers grow to be not more than thirty inches long. They are sleek, low-slung (Corvette-like) ground dwellers. As nocturnal prowlers, they are seldom seen. Badgers are fierce fighters with powerful jaws; long, sharp teeth; and two-inch claws. Extremely rugged and resilient, they can whip creatures up to four times their size!

However, they are great at bluffing their opponents. A badger stands, snarling and arching its back . . . but at the precise moment it is about to get caught or chewed up and spit out, it suddenly retreats!

Here's how: Badgers are unlike all other animals whose hair is "set" in such a manner that it lies in only one direction. Remember how we can rub a cat "the wrong way" or do the same with a dog? Not so with a badger! Badgers' hair can go *both* ways. Its skin is so loose and its hair so thick and flexible that another creature can't get a good grip on it. This makes a badger the classic *escape artist!* When confronted, it may choose to fight. More often, however, (being clever) it will choose to retreat.

Now, we're beginning to uncover a clue in this list of small creatures. Both the ant, which can slip into an anthill, and the badger, which escapes when confronted, are good illustrations of one of man's (and woman's!) favorite indoor sports: *making excuses*. Some get so good at it, no one can get a grip on them. It may appear to be small and insignificant as weaknesses go, but excuse-making can take a heavy toll. Active spirituality, on the other hand, should never be accused of such irresponsible behavior.

The Locust

We're getting smaller again. This insect is about the size of a grasshopper. They may have "no king" (unlike Canadian geese in flight, or a pride of lions on a savanna which follow a definite leader); nevertheless, locusts are a team that can "go out in ranks." The gregarious locust swarm can wreck havoc on endless miles of crops. Interestingly, they can be mild and quiet, then suddenly become restless and irritable. They can turn in their moods and suddenly become violent, taking flight and traveling incredible distances.

Some swarms sound like a huge commercial jetliner overhead. And when they have finished with their attack on crops, every plant—every single plant—is stripped down to a barren, bleeding stalk, as if a fire had swept across the scene. One particular swarm was spotted as far as twelve hundred miles out at sea, flying northward from West Africa toward the British Isles. Another swarm covered a breadth of air space no less than two thousand square miles.

Amazing creature, the locust . . . and how moody! Quiet and placid, yet within moments, irritable and restless.

The Lizard

According to this saying, we're able to grasp the lizard with our hands, yet it is ever so slippery. The next thing we know, it winds up "in kings' palaces." How? Well, that's the lizard's secret; it's a master of disguises. It can blend in so perfectly with its background, no one even notices its presence. Operation camouflage. Slippery when grabbed, it squirts away, and to everyone's surprise, it shows up elsewhere in all its glory!

Ants, badgers, locusts, and lizards present a small but very clever message to all who live with excuses and don't take responsible action. We can easily escape, slip away, change our moods, and go right on without accepting or even acknowledging the confrontation. When we do these things we become totally irresponsible. The devastation of living like that can be enormous. For example, those who continue to live financially irresponsible lives often wind up declaring bankruptcy. Or husbands and wives who prefer to overlook their part in marital conflicts go from one marriage to the next with little change in their habits. Fortunately, however, taking responsibility can solve conflicts; it can lessen or eliminate the undesirable consequences.

The ant, despite its smallness, is wise enough to prepare its food in the summer. The badger, despite its not being mighty, is wise enough to make its house in the rocks. The locus, despite having no leader, can move out in ranks. The lizard, despite its changeability, is found in kings' palaces. These creatures are complex, like us. They have qualities which are undesirable, but they also have qualities that make them "exceedingly wise." We humans are blessed with the ability to choose, to emphasize or deemphasize qualities within us.

This is a good time to take a straight look at your tendency to dodge the hard questions . . . to ignore the warnings of a friend . . . to slip from the grip of one whose criticism may hurt at the moment, but later could prove extremely beneficial. Honestly now . . .

- Are you firm or slippery?
- How about stable and open or moody and evasive?
- Is it your tendency to be honest or to bluff?
- Do you enjoy showing what's there or camouflage?
- Have you a favorite quiet place for prayer and listening for guidance or an anthill of escape?
- Does confrontation sometimes seem appropriate or does it annoy or frighten you?

Active spirituality works hard at coming to terms with an excuse-making lifestyle. Living responsibly starts with facing up to the truth and making wise choices.

Spirituality in Action

∽ Which creature are you more like (and consider both aspects of each):

The ant? Why?
The badger? In what way?
The locust? How?
The lizard? Explain.

∽ Think of situations where you most often feel the need to slip away and run. See if you can detect a familiar pattern—a recurring scene. Now for the tough one: *Why?* What makes you so hard to nail down? Is there something to hide? Something you fear? Are you afraid to let others get close? What's the reason behind that pattern? What are your alternatives?

∽ No relationships are more significant to our development than those of early childhood. It is during those years that we form our first habits in handling life situations. Reflect back:

• Was your mother or father moody?
• Was evasiveness permitted? Modeled?
• Can you recall how confrontation may have

been mishandled back then?
- Were you taught to live without accountability?
- Did you develop excuse-making in your early years?

Discuss this with a few friends. Be vulnerable. Talk openly about your ant-badger-locust-lizard makeup and consider your options.

~

20

Financial Accountability

Honor the Lord from your wealth,
And from the first of all your produce;
So your barns will be filled with plenty,
And your vats will overflow with new wine. (3:9–10)

∽ ∽ ∽

It is the blessing of the Lord that makes rich,
And He adds no sorrow to it. (10:22)

∽ ∽ ∽

How much better it is to get wisdom than gold!
And to get understanding is to be chosen
  above silver. (16:16)

∽ ∽ ∽

Do not weary yourself to gain wealth,
Cease from your consideration of it.
When you set your eyes on it, it is gone.
For wealth certainly makes itself wings,
Like an eagle that flies toward the heavens. (23:4–5)

∽ ∽ ∽

He who tills his land will have plenty of food,
But he who follows empty pursuits will have
  poverty in plenty.
A faithful man will abound with blessings,
But he who makes haste to be rich will not
  be unpunished. (28:19–20)

❂ FEW CHALLENGES in our culture are more ambiguous and energy-draining than those related to financial responsibility. Our culture presents many temptations, many images of "the good life." Many are the headaches and heartaches of striving for that "good life." Great are the worries of those, for example, who continue to increase their indebtedness or spend impulsively or loan money to others indiscriminately. Being accountable with money is of primary concern to the spiritually active individual.

To such Christians, the sayings of Solomon you just read bring a sting to the conscience, especially if they describe your situation. What's worse, they may describe where you have found yourself off and on for as long as you can remember. It may not bring much comfort to know that *you are not alone,* but there is perhaps no more common problem among Americans than this one. So common is it that places of business must protect themselves from this phenomenon by operating under strict guidelines. All this reminds me of a sign that made me smile. It hangs in a Fort Lauderdale restaurant:

IF YOU ARE OVER 80 YEARS OLD
AND ACCOMPANIED BY YOUR PARENTS,
WE WILL CASH YOUR CHECK

Some wag once described our times with three different definitions:

Recession: When the man next door loses his job.
Depression: When you lose your job.
Panic: When your wife loses her job.

Many families have reached the place where the wife's working is no longer an optional luxury, it's a necessity.

To the surprise of no one, the sayings of Scripture having to do with money are numerous. Long before Ben Franklin penned his wit and wisdom in *Poor Richard's Almanac,* Solomon's words had been around for centuries, available for all to read. When you attempt to categorize them, you realize just how varied the subjects are that have to do with financial matters. You also see how much good practical advise they contain.

Solomon's sayings cover a broad spectrum, including getting money (earning and inheriting), releasing money (spending, squandering, loaning, and giving), investing money, saving money, and handling money wisely. The synonyms used in Scripture are many: money, wealth, riches, lending, borrowing, spending, giving, losing, silver, gold, plenty, abundance, want, poverty, and a half dozen others.

Having traced the subject through Solomon's sayings, I have discovered the following principles of financial accountability that should characterize your spiritual pilgrimage in this area. There are six of them.

1   *Those who honor God with their money are blessed in return.*

> Honor the Lord from your wealth,
> And from the first of all your produce;
> So your barns will be filled with plenty,
> And your vats will overflow with new
>   wine. (3:9–10)

> It is the blessing of the Lord that makes rich,
> And He adds no sorrow to it. (10:22)
> Adversity pursues sinners,
> But the righteous will be rewarded with
>   prosperity. (13:21)

I have said for years that you can tell much more about an individual's dedication to God by looking at that person's checkbook than by looking at his or her Bible. Again and again throughout Scripture, we read of the blessings God grants (not all of them tangible, by the way) to those who "honor the Lord" with their finances.

2   *Those who make riches their passion lose much more*
    than they gain.

> Do not weary yourself to gain wealth,
> Cease from your consideration of it.
> When you set your eyes on it, it is gone.
> For wealth certainly makes itself wings,
> Like an eagle that flies toward the heavens. (23:4–5)

Can't you just picture the scene? For that reason I think it is appropriate that an eagle appears on much of our American currency! Who hasn't been tempted by some get-rich-quick scheme? And think of the thousands of people who are drawn into the broad and juicy appeal of the investors who promise they can make a killing for them on their "deal." Beware of words like "it's a once-in-a-lifetime" opportunity! Another that ought to make us cringe: "This is too good to be true." (It usually is!) When you hear such stuff, listen for the flapping of eagles' wings. And heed instead the wisdom of Solomon's words!

> He who tills his land will have plenty of food,
> But he who follows empty pursuits will have
>   poverty in plenty.
> A faithful man will abound with blessings,
> But he who makes haste to be rich will not be
>   unpunished. (28:19–20)

A man with an evil eye hastens after wealth,

> And does not know that want will come upon
> him. (28:22)

3 *Wisdom gives wealth guidance.* If you have a choice
between wisdom and wealth, count on it; *wisdom*
is much to be preferred!

> Take my instruction, and not silver,
> And knowledge rather than choicest gold.
> For wisdom is better than jewels;
> And all desirable things can not compare
> with her. (8:10–11)

> Riches and honor are with me,
> Enduring wealth and righteousness.
> My fruit is better than gold, even pure gold,
> And my yield than choicest silver. (8:18–19)

> How much better it is to get wisdom than gold!
> And to get understanding is to be chosen above
> silver. (16:16)

Wisdom (active spirituality at work) provides
the recipient of increased finances with the restraints that are needed. Furthermore, it helps one
maintain that essential equilibrium, for much
wealth can be a heady trip. Since riches never made
anyone honest or generous or discerning, wisdom
must come aboard to steer our vessel around those
disastrous shallow reefs. The reason for this brings
us to a fourth principle of financial responsibility.

4 *Increased riches bring increased complications.* As I

examine the biblical record, I find several such complications mentioned in the Book of Proverbs:

- A false sense of security

    The rich man's wealth is his fortress,
    The ruin of the poor is their poverty. (10:15)

    A rich man's wealth is his strong city,
    And like a high wall in his own imagination. (18:11)

- A sudden burst of many new "friends"

    The poor is hated even by his neighbor,
    But those who love the rich are many. (14:20)

    Wealth adds many friends,
    But a poor man is separated from his friend. (19:4)

    A man of many friends comes to ruin,
    But there is a friend who sticks closer than a
        brother. (18:24)

- The possibility of arrogance and pride

    The poor man utters supplications,
    But the rich man answers roughly. (18:23)

    The rich man is wise in his own eyes,
    But the poor who has understanding sees through
        him. (28:11)

- Increased moral temptations

    Do not desire her beauty in your heart,
    Nor let her catch you with her eyelids.

For on account of a harlot one is reduced to a loaf
  of bread,
And an adulteress hunts for the precious life.
Can a man take fire in his bosom,
And his clothes not be burned?
Or can a man walk on hot coals,
And his feet not be scorched? (6:25–28)

A man who loves wisdom makes his father glad,
But he who keeps company with harlots wastes his
  wealth. (29:3)

5   *Money cannot buy life's most valuable possessions.*

It is strange how so many live under the delusion
that a fat bank account will make possible "the best
things in life" when, in fact, it will provide no such
thing. Don't misunderstand. There is nothing
wrong with having wealth if it has been earned
honestly and if one's perspective stays clear. However, "the good life" should not be equated with
"the true life," which Paul calls "life indeed"
(1 Timothy 6:19) and what I've termed "active spirituality". Money will only buy things that are for sale
. . . and happiness or a clear conscience or freedom
from worry is not among them. Money can be used
to purchase lovely and comfortable dwellings, pleasure vacations, and delightful works of art. But the
priceless things in life are not for sale.

What are some of those priceless possessions?

• Peace

Better is a little with the fear of the Lord,
Than great treasure and turmoil with it. (15:16)

- Love

Better is a dish of vegetables where love is,
Than a fattened ox and hatred with it. (15:17)

  - A good name . . . reputation and respect

A good name is to be more desired than great
  riches,
Favor is better than silver and gold. (22:1)

- Integrity

Better is the poor who walks in his integrity,
Than he who is crooked though he be rich. (28:6)

6 *If handled wisely, money can be the means of great
   encouragement, but if mishandled, great stress.*

Adversity pursues sinners,
But the righteous will be rewarded with prosperity.
A good man leaves an inheritance to his children's
  children,
And the wealth of the sinner is stored up for the
  righteous. (13:21–22)

Who can measure the encouragement our
money can bring to others? If reared correctly, our
children can benefit from and know the joy of re-
ceiving an inheritance from their parents. God's
Word admonishes parents to provide for their fami-

lies. Ministries of every kind are dependent upon the financial generosity of those who support them. The hungry can be fed, the poor can be clothed, the homeless can be sheltered, the abused can be comforted, the untaught can be educated . . . the list of possibilities is endless.

There is the flip side, however:

The rich rules over the poor,
And the borrower becomes the lender's
   slave. (22:7)

Do not be among those who give pledges,
Among those who become sureties for debts.
If you have nothing with which to pay,
Why should he take your bed from under
   you? (22:26–27)

This hardly needs to be explained. Pause over those key words . . . especially *slave*. No other term better describes the feeling of being financially unaccountable. Never let anyone tell you that slavery has been abolished. It's worldwide!

If this happens to be a troubled area in your life, let me encourage you to ignore it no longer. No more excuses! There are too many helpful books and reliable resources available for you showing how to proceed in a responsible and accountable manner. Begin the process of change this week.

SPIRITUALITY IN ACTION

૭ Select three or four from the many sayings about money matters you just read that speak most pointedly to you. Write them on separate three-by-five cards and commit them to memory. You might also tape one of them on the front of your checkbook! Reflect on the truth of what you are committing to memory. Use those truths in several conversations in the coming days.

૭ One of the most helpful, practical tools you can use in getting a handle on your money is a budget. Establish a simple and easy-to-follow personal budget. If you need help, ask someone you respect for advice. If that person cannot help, surely he or she can steer you in the right direction by referring you to help from another source. Write down a realistic financial game plan you will put in motion.

૭ There are several splendid books available today on the subject of handling money wisely. There are also seminars and conferences, plus audio and video tapes provided by reliable authorities in the field of finances. You can take a giant step toward achieving financial responsibility by doing one (or more) of three things:

• Purchase and begin reading a book on money

management.
- Listen to a set of tapes on the subject.
- Look into a financial seminar that would best meet your need and make definite plans to attend. If you are married, go as a couple. The road that leads to domestic financial accountability is a two–way street.

21

Pleasing God

There are six things which the Lord hates,
Yes, seven which are an abomination to Him:
Haughty eyes, a lying tongue,
And hands that shed innocent blood.
A heart that devises wicked plans,
Feet that run rapidly to evil,
A false witness who utters lies,
And one who spreads strife among
  brothers. (6:16–19)

✪ EVEN THOUGH WE have mentioned various shades of this subject and have glanced at these sayings on more than one occasion in our study together, we need to face the music directly. Who hasn't struggled daily with the idea that they have not pleased the Lord? Is there an area that brings greater ache of soul? I don't think so.

The active spiritual Christian does not begin the day thinking about how he (or she) might displease God. On the contrary, such people usually face the dawn with high hopes of pleasing Him. In our minds we establish a game plan that will include a good attitude, a day of wholesome activities. We prepare ourselves for possible temptations and trials by meeting early with our God and giving Him our day in advance. And yet . . . before the morning is half done, we can fall into a syndrome of carnality that is downright discouraging, if not altogether demoralizing.

Perhaps it will help us to focus in on a specific target. Rather than praying in general terms, "Lord, help me to please You," it may be more beneficial to name seven specific areas where we need help. The list of seven is inspired—Solomon calls them the "seven which are an abomination" to our Lord. At the end of each of the seven discussions that follow, you will find a suggested prayer.

1 *Haughty eyes.* Our eyes reveal the truth of our souls. They convey so many of our unspoken emotions. Eyes announce anger, impatience, fear, sorrow, sarcasm, guilt, shame, and especially pride. It's that last one God hates with intensity.

   "God, guard me all this week from hidden arrogance!"

2 *A lying tongue.* Not all lies are big and bold. Half-truths flow so freely. Exaggerations, too. And false words of flattery are commonly heard. Since we looked at the tongue so closely in chapters eight and nine, have you been more conscious of your words? Are you more aware of the power your tongue possesses?

   "God, alert me to the destructive force of my tongue. Stop me from every form of lying!"

3 *Hands that shed innocent blood.* Solomon clearly states that the Lord considers murder an abomination. You may have been victimized by someone. It could be going on right now. As time passes, unless forgiveness replaces resentment, your bitterness could grow into rage . . . and you could "shed inno-

cent blood." You may have a major battle with abusing your child. If so, you must get help!

"God, direct me to wholesome and healthy ways to solve and dissolve my uncontrolled anger. Keep me from the sin of shedding innocent blood!"

4   *A heart that devises wicked plans.* Because we have examined the heart so carefully, we are aware of its power and its importance. Nothing we do or say occurs until it has been filtered through the heart within us. It is there that "wicked plans" are laid. It is there we map out our yielding to temptation, our release of restraint, our impulsive urge to spend irresponsibly, our scheme to get even with someone else.

"God, cleanse my heart from any hurtful way . . . remove every ugly thought or wicked scheme I have been pondering!"

5   *Feet that run rapidly to evil.* Old habits are hard to break. Because we have "gotten away with it" before, the skids of sin are greased. In fact, we become increasingly less fearful of God's stepping in the longer we get away with continued, familiar paths of sin. "Because God does not punish sinners instantly, people feel it is safe to do wrong" (Eccles. 8:11, TLB).

"God, halt me in my tracks!"

6   *A false witness who utters lies.* Rare are the truth

tellers. Many are those who deliberately misrepresent the facts. When we have the opportunity to defend another's character or set the record straight in a group that is bad-mouthing a certain individual, the temptation to chime in and agree (or remain silent and allow the character assassination to continue) is great. But the Lord hates such actions.

"God, free me from whatever fears I have so that my witness will be true, based on accurate facts!"

7 *One who spreads strife among brothers.* Juicy information is so difficult to contain. This is especially true if there is an element of verbal malignancy in the talk. How easy to "spread strife" among our brothers and sisters . . . how hard to be a peacemaker! But Solomon pulls no punches. He calls this one of those abominations God despises. This is the third in the list having to do with the tongue.

"God, silence me from any act of slander or even a hint of gossip!"

We frequently think of the love of God, but all too seldom meditate on the things He hates. We should! Believe me, when God's Word says He hates these things, there is intensity in the statement. That means each one deserves an intensity of our effort to correct and control the wrongs that are named. As people committed to an active spiritual life, we can do no less.

SPIRITUALITY IN ACTION

∾ Go back to the closing prayers in each of the seven areas mentioned in the sayings. Interestingly, there are seven specific things God hates . . . one for each day in the week. You can probably anticipate this project. On a Sunday, take that first subject area on God's "hate list" (*haughty eyes*) and pray the prayer I've suggested throughout the day. Concentrate on overcoming that all day Sunday. On Monday, take the second; Tuesday, the third . . . follow the plan all week long.

∾ Since three of these seven have to do with the tongue, we must give great attention to this powerful force. Pay special attention not only to what you say but how and when you say it . . . and why . . . and to whom. Talk less and say more.

∾ Which one thing mentioned in the list could be called your most frequent battleground? Be absolutely relentless as you roll up your sleeves and take on this hateful, ugly enemy of righteousness. Displeasing God is habit-forming! But so can be our pleasing Him. Tell at least two other people of your major struggle. Request their prayers. Trust God to use their intercession and your concentrated effort to defeat this enemy.

22

Gaining Wisdom

The proverbs of Solomon the son of David,
  king of Israel:
To know wisdom and instruction,
To discern the sayings of understanding,
To receive instruction in wise behavior,
Righteousness, justice and equity;
To give prudence to the naïve,
To the youth knowledge and discretion,
A wise man will hear and increase in learning,
And a man of understanding will acquire
  wise counsel,
To understand a proverb and a figure,
The words of the wise and their riddles.
The fear of the Lord is the beginning of knowledge;
Fools despise wisdom and instruction.
Hear, my son, your father's instruction,
And do not forsake your mother's teaching;
Indeed, they are a graceful wreath to your head,
And ornaments about your neck.
My son, if sinners entice you,
Do not consent.
If they say, "Come with us,
Let us lie in wait for blood,
Let us ambush the innocent without cause;

Let us swallow them alive like Sheol,
Even whole, as those who go down to the pit;
We shall find all kinds of precious wealth,
We shall fill our houses with spoil;
Throw in your lot with us,
We shall all have one purse."
My son do not walk in the way with them.
Keep your feet from their path,
For their feet run to evil,
And they hasten to shed blood.
Indeed, it is useless to spread the net
In the eyes of any bird;
But they lie in wait for their own blood;
They ambush their own lives.
So are the ways of everyone who gains by violence;
It takes away the life of its possessors.
Wisdom shouts in the street,
She lifts her voice in the square;
At the head of the noisy streets she cries out;
At the entrance of the gates in the city, she utters
    her sayings:
"How long, O naïve ones, will you love simplicity?
And scoffers delight themselves in scoffing,
And fools hate knowledge?
Turn to my reproof,
Behold, I will pour out my spirit on you;
I will make my words known to you." (1:1–23)

❀ WHEN WE FIRST looked at the sayings of Scripture we began with the first chapter of Proverbs. It occurs to me that it would be worthwhile to return to it for a final time as we consider this vital point: *active spirituality values wisdom over knowledge.* If there is one key lesson to be learned from this book, this is it. But beware, the tendency to do just the opposite is a life-long struggle.

How easy it is to acquire knowledge, yet how difficult and painstaking is the process of gaining wisdom. Man gives knowledge; God gives wisdom. Knowledge is gleaned from getting an education—either by listening to and reading what the learned have to say or simply by gathering facts here and yon from your own experience. But what about the wisdom that is from above? As you already know, there is no course, no knowledge which can be measured in objective analyses and IQ tests and rewarded with diplomas and degrees. Wisdom defies measurement; it is much more subjective, takes far more time, and has a great deal to do with attitude. One can be knowledgeable yet inactive—distant from the living God—living a passive, mostly contemplative spiritual life. But those who are wise not only know the Lord by faith in His Son, Jesus Christ, they also hold Him in awesome respect which results in their wanting to be actively involved in His kingdom's work here on earth. "The fear of the Lord" remains a timeless telltale mark of wisdom.

So how does one obtain wisdom? Now that we have come to an end of our search through the sayings of Scripture, how can we continue our pursuit of God's wisdom? What are some ways to guard against falling back into our habit of substituting knowledge for wisdom?

I have four thoughts to suggest:

1   *Read the Book of Proverbs regularly.*

> The proverbs of Solomon the son of David,
>   king of Israel:
> To know wisdom and instruction,
> To discern the sayings of understanding,
> To receive instruction in wise behavior,
> Righteousness, justice and equity;
> To give prudence to the naïve,
> To the youth knowledge and discretion,
> A wise man will hear and increase in learning,
> And a man of understanding will acquire wise
>   counsel,
> To understand a proverb and a figure,
> The words of the wise and their riddles.

The fear of the Lord is the beginning of knowledge;
Fools despise wisdom and instruction. (1–7)

The Book of Proverbs has thirty-one chapters—a natural fit into each month. It includes descriptions of over 180 different types of people. There is no mumbo-jumbo, no Rubic's-cube theology to unscramble, no weird, abstract theories to unravel, only straight talk for all of us who live imperfect lives on Planet Earth. Since Solomon declares that his writings have been recorded to help us "know wisdom," I suggest we take him up on it and glean new dimensions of wisdom by sitting at his feet. Read one chapter of the Book of Proverbs every day for the rest of your life and chances are good you'll not often be tempted to substitute knowledge for wisdom.

2   *Hear and heed the counsel of those you respect.*

Hear, my son, your father's instruction,
And do not forsake your mother's teaching;
Indeed, they are a graceful wreath to your head,
And ornaments about your neck. (8–9)

Wisdom isn't limited to the sayings of Scripture. It is possible that God has given you a godly set of parents, several trusted mentors, and one or two wise friends. They have been through experiences and endured some trials you have not yet encountered. They have had time to weave all that through the varied fabrics of life, which gives them a discernment and depth you may lack. The things they can pass along to you are "a graceful wreath . . . and ornaments" of wisdom available to you. Listen to them. Learn from them. Linger with them.

3   *Choose your friends carefully.*

> My son, if sinners entice you,
> Do not consent.
> If they say, "Come with us,
> Let us lie in wait for blood,
> Let us ambush the innocent without cause;
> Let us swallow them alive like Sheol,
> Even whole, as those who go down to the pit;
> We shall find all kinds of precious wealth,
> We shall fill our houses with spoil;
> Throw in your lot with us,
> We shall have one purse,
> My son do not walk in the way with them.
> Keep your feet from their path,
> For their feet run to evil,
> And they hasten to shed blood.
> Indeed, it is useless to spread the net
> In the eyes of any bird;
> But they lie in wait for their own blood;
> They ambush their own lives.
> So are the ways of everyone who gains by violence;
> It takes away the life of its possessors. (10–19)

The longer I live the more careful I am with my choice of friends. I have fewer than in my youthful years, but they are deeper friends . . . treasured relationships.

As we read in Solomon's counsel, do not consent to relationships that drag you down and hurt your walk with God. Those who "ambush their own lives" (v. 18) will get you involved in counterproductive activities that will keep wisdom at arm's distance. You don't need that.

4 *Pay close attention to life's reproofs.*

> Wisdom shouts in the street,
> She lifts her voice in the square;
> At the head of the noisy streets she cries out;
> At the entrance of the gates in the city, she utters
>   her sayings:
> "How long, O naïve ones, will you love
>   simplicity?
> And scoffers delight themselves in scoffing.
> And fools hate knowledge?
> Turn to my reproof,
> Behold, I will pour out my spirit on you;
> I will make my words known to you." (20–23)

If you have been on this journey since the beginning, perhaps you recall the time we spent analyzing these words. Wisdom is personified as one who "shouts in the street" and "lifts her voice in the square." In other words, she is available. She speaks loud and clear. But, where? How? She tells us! "Turn to my reproof." It is there (in life's reproofs) she pours out her spirit on us and makes her words known to us.

God never wastes our time, allowing us to go through the dark and dismal valleys or endure those winding, painful paths without purpose. In each one there are "reproofs" with wisdom attached. Many and foolish are those who simply grit their teeth and bear it. Few but wise are those who hear wisdom's voice and listen to her counsel.

The wisdom-filled life is the actively spiritual life. For the rest of our years on this old earth, let's do our best to be numbered among this group.

SPIRITUALITY IN ACTION

∾ As we have discovered through the course of this book, the secret of memory is review, review, review. Today is a good day to set up a plan for reviewing the sayings of Solomon. If you wish to read through the Book of Proverbs on a daily basis, think about the best time and place for doing so. To keep the readings fresh, you might want to pick up a copy of the Scriptures in a different version or perhaps a paraphrase. As you read through the Book of Proverbs, you may also want to review some of the pertinent discussions in this book.

∾ All of us have at least one wise person we really admire—a genuinely mature, spiritually active person. If at all possible, arrange a time to get together . . . perhaps once a month or once every other month. If that won't work, how about listening to audio tapes that person has made or reading some things he (or she) has written? You may find that cultivating a close companionship and accountability with a small group of trusted friends is the best way to fulfill your desire for a spiritually active lifestyle.

∾ As a final, end-of-the-book project, bow and thank the Lord for His faithfulness to you. His Word has been our guide. His mercy and grace, our encouragement. His love, our motivation. His Spirit, our Helper. His power to bring about changes within us, our hope. Express to Him how grateful you are for all He has taught you in these pages and for His patience with you as you attempt to grow spiritually.

∾

Conclusion

❀ As we have journeyed through the book of Proverbs to gain a picture of active spirituality at work, I hope you have learned as much as I have! In the process of gleaning truth, encouragement, insight, and growing spiritually, I hope you have come to know yourself better—a better understanding of one's self is always a byproduct of time spend in God's relevant revelation.

Most of all, however, I hope you have come to know our Lord in new and fresh ways—and have discovered that He is vitally interested in the nuts and bolts of your everyday existence. In fact, it seems there is nothing He is not interested in, certainly nothing He is not aware of! If He has the hair on our heads numbered, He must care intimately and intensely about the things that concern us . . . especially our daily spiritual walk.

My objective all along has been twofold: first, to provide you with comments and explanations of selected proverbs so you could see the relationship between wisdom and active spirituality; and second, to assist you with applications and suggestions of each so you could put the truth into action.

Nothing would please me more than to know that my objective was accomplished, namely, that you have grown spiritually in your understanding of these immortal proverbs and that you have begun to turn that knowledge into active spirituality in practical ways.

I must confess to you that when I began to write this book, I looked upon the assignment with a heavy sigh. The journey before me seemed long and arduous—not a very "spiritual" process I whispered to myself. I found myself struggling with (occasionally even *dreading*!) the task. But what a pleasant surprise awaited me!

The more I got into the work, the greater became my motivation. But the real miracle was how I, personally, grew spiritually through the process. To tell you the truth, it wasn't long before I could hardly sleep due to my excitement. Ideas came with increasing, sometimes furious, speed. It got to the place where I could not write fast enough! The time spent in these words of wisdom from God's truth became the highlight of my day. I realize now that I was being given a literal illustration of the message of this book. What I first saw as a demanding, pressing assignment God turned into a joyful, fulfilling, and growing experience. This "Non-devotional Guide" has become the motivation for some very personal growth!

Active spirituality is full of such serendipities. What we dread, He is able to transform . . . and frequently *does*! What we lack in energy or ability, He supplies in abundance. What we alone are unable to handle, He handles for us—His helping hand makes up the difference. The book you hold in your hands is a tangible proof of what you just read.

I am smiling as I write these concluding words; to my own surprise I have been the first recipient of blessing from this project. The sayings I had hoped would help you have helped me already. The reflections that I felt might be of encouragement to you have become encouraging me for weeks. Of this I am certain: they work!

Now I can say beyond the shadow of a doubt that the wisdom of active spirituality is reliable truth. It is, in fact, the life God has designed for us to live. That is why He gets all the glory.

~

Notes

1   Augustine, *Confessions*, cited in *The Great Thoughts*, compiled
    by George Seldez (NY: Ballantine, 1985), 25.

2   Karl Menninger in *The Chosen* by Chaim Potok (frontis-
    piece). A Fawcett Crest Book, published by Ballantine Books.
    Copyright 1967 by Chaim Potok.

≈

∾

ACTIVE SPIRITUALITY was designed by Mark McGarry & has been set entirely in Minion by the typesetting department of Word Publishing. Designed for digital composition by Robert Slimbach, Minion echoes the best of the later Renaissance typefaces. The printer & binder was Berryville Graphics, Berryville, Virginia.

The Hebrew text that adorns each chapter title page is taken from Solomon's *Proverbs*, chapter one, verses one & following. In keeping with early scribal practices, the characters appear in their unpointed form, with no extra space between words.

∾